GIRLHOOD DAYS

Fourth in the series
MEMORIES OF
HOOSIER HOMEMAKERS

Eleanor Arnold
Editor and Project Director

F. Gerald Handfield Jr.
Oral History Consultant

Paul Wilson
Photographic Consultant

From Hoosier Homemakers Through The Years
an oral history project of
The Indiana Extension Homemakers Association

First Indiana University Press edition 1995

The paper used in this publication meets the minimum requirements of
American National Standard for Information Sciences—Permanence of
Paper for Printed Library Materials, ANSI Z39.48-1984.

⊗™

Manufactured in the United States of America

Library of Congress Cataloging-in-Publication Data

Memories of Hoosier homemakers / Eleanor Arnold, editor and project
director.
p. cm.
''From Hoosier Homemakers Through the Years, an oral history
project of the Indiana Extension Homemakers Association.''
Originally published: [West Lafayette?] : Indiana Extension
Homemakers Association, c1983–1990.
Contents: 1st. Feeding our families — 2nd. Party lines, pumps,
and privies — 3rd. Buggies and bad times — 4th. Girlhood days —
5th. Going to club — 6th. Living rich lives — [7th] Index.
Includes indexes.
ISBN 0-253-12994-X (set). — ISBN 0-253-20807-6 (pbk. : set). —
ISBN 0-253-12992-3 (v. 1). — ISBN 0-253-20805-X (pbk. : v. 1). —
ISBN 0-253-12987-7 (v. 2). — ISBN 0-253-20800-9 (pbk. : v. 2). —
ISBN 0-253-12991-5 (v. 3). — ISBN 0-253-20804-1 (pbk. : v. 3). —
ISBN 0-253-12989-3 (v. 4). — ISBN 0-253-20802-5 (pbk. : v. 4). —
ISBN 0-253-12990-7 (v. 5). — ISBN 0-253-20803-3 (pbk. : v. 5). —
ISBN 0-253-12988-5 (v. 6). — ISBN 0-253-20801-7 (pbk. : v. 6). —
ISBN 0-253-20806-8 (pbk. : v. 7)
1. Home economics, Rural—Indiana—History—Sources. 2. Rural
women—Indiana—History—Sources. 3. Indiana—Social life and
customs—History—Sources. I. Arnold, Eleanor. II. Indiana
Extension Homemakers Association. III. Hoosier Homemakers Through
the Years (Project)
TX24.I6M46   1985a
640'.9772 — dc20   93-13283

1 2 3 4 5 6 7 8 99 98 97 96 95

Front Cover
Two happy farm girls play
in a straw stack.
Submitted by Newton County

TABLE OF CONTENTS

"I enjoy thinking back over the years
that I lived out on the farm
and I get to thinking about it.
I think I'd like to go back just for one more day
and listen to the old red rooster crowing
from the top of the garden fence. I'd like to hear
the old henhouse come alive, and
I'd like to hear the cowbell tinkle as she come up
the cow path every evening with our daily milk.
And I'd like to lay up in the old loft in the hay
and listen to the raindrops on the old tin roof
while I read a book and dream away the day.

And I'd like to go with my mother one more time
down the cow path and pick a gallon of
big ripe juicy blackberries and eat the cobbler
she'd bake in the big old family baking pan.
And I'd like to go back to the schoolhouse
and I'd like to play the games we'd play at school
when we were litte.

I'd like to go to a taffy pulling once more,
and I'd like to have the old-fashioned husking bees
where we gathered around in the evening.
What a time we had!"

Alvah Watson, 97, Allen County

PREFACE

The Project

This book is the fourth in a series called Memories of Hoosier Homemakers. A brief explanation may be helpful in understanding both this book and the overall scope of the project.

In 1988 Indiana Extension Homemakers Association will celebrate the 75th anniversary of their founding. The IEHA is a statewide organization which serves as the audience group of the Cooperative Extension Service of Purdue University with a membership numbering 30,000. Anticipating this birthday, an oral history project was initiated which has interviewed 235 homemakers all over Indiana. Funded by the Indiana Committee for the Humanities in its initial stages and staffed by dedicated volunteers, the project has been hugely successful in documenting women in their role as homemakers.

This book deals with the women's memories of their lives as they grew up in a primarily rural or small-town atmosphere. The first book of the series, *Feeding Our Families,* recorded the women's involvement with food in raising, harvesting, preserving, cooking and serving food. The second book, *Party Lines, Pumps and Privies,* dealt with the changes technology has made in homemaking chores. The third book, *Buggies and Bad Times,* discussed two subjects—changes in transportation, from buggies to airplanes; and the impact of world events on the homes and how the women dealt with these impacts.

Two more books are planned in the series. The next, to be published in the anniversary year, will be the women's memories of the organization and of their participation in it. The last culminating volume will focus on their lives as women, their family relationships and their judgments on their lives.

The collection of related visual materials has resulted in a slide/tape program *Hoosier Homemakers; the Early Years* which has been widely viewed. This collection, together with the interview tapes and transcriptions, is housed in the Indiana Historical Society.

Everyone concerned with the project has been extremely gratified by its achievements in documenting the homemaker's role, and by the success of its products.

EDITOR'S NOTES

A few notes may aid the reader's understanding of the way this book has been edited. The book is composed entirely, aside from editorial comment, of words taken from the project interviews. My task, as editor, was to select these words and place them in order, so that the experiences of many women could become a coherent whole.

In order to make the sense of the interview clear, I had to omit false starts and repetitions and, in some cases, have had to cut extraneous material for the sake of brevity and coherence. The words, however, are the words they spoke.

Occasional words or phrases will be found in brackets[ ]. Here I have added something to clarify the excerpt or to explain the meaning of a word which might be unfamiliar.

Words in bold type are the words of the person conducting the interview and those in regular type are the words of the narrator. In the back of the book is a list of interviewers and interviewees, listed by counties, so that the interested reader may find who has conducted any interview.

The name following the excerpt is the name of the person who is talking. Her age at the time of the interview and her county are included to help the reader place the era and locale from which her memories came. A map of Indiana inside the back cover shows the location of the counties.

Visual material in the book came from materials collected by and from the homemakers, unless otherwise noted. Some photographs are from the collection of J. C. Allen, who was staff photographer at Purdue University for many years and did extensive coverage of extension activities.

Eleanor Arnold
Editor and Project Director
R.R. 2, Box 48
Rushville, IN 46173
317/932-5204

INTRODUCTION

The previous books in the Memories of Hoosier Homemakers series have dealt with different facets of our narrator's adult lives, as will the ones to follow. This book, however, looks at the years which shaped the adult women—their growing up years.

Our narrators varied in age, in family background and in the locale of their homes, but the majority are recalling young lives lived in rural and small-town settings somewhere between the years of 1890 to 1940.

The physical boundaries of these lives were small, limited by the transportation and communication available at the time. One narrator recalls the world was seven miles long each way. Seven miles to Grandma's, going east; and seven miles to their shopping town, going west. Another child watched the boats on the Ohio River and remembers, "We thought they came from nowhere and were going into another world." Therefore, their reported experiences lie close to home.

The family unit was very strong, led by parents whose lives were dedicated to their family. By necessity, the members of the family spent most of their time together, either working together or attending and participating in community activities together.

Meals were eaten together, preceded by prayer, and stairsteps of children walked off to school together, where they recited in each other's hearing in the one-room school and played in each other's sight at recess.

The size of the family unit necessitated hard physical labor by all members. Even very small children had necessary chores which had to be performed without fail. Children of 10 or 12 years of age might be working almost as hard as an adult, with corresponding worries and responsibilities. However, each child was very aware that his contribution was essential to the family welfare.

The moral precepts and values of the home and community were very high. A strong religious atmosphere was general in the nation at this time, and the rural areas were particularly God-fearing.

The Sabbath day was strictly observed, with Sunday School and church on Sunday morning and the rest of the day given over to social gatherings and/or rest, with only the necessary farm chores being done. To children who had been hard at work, either at home or at school, Sundays were eagerly anticipated. The neighborhood was full of children, and they gathered to participate in simple activities together.

The young people of the era were keenly interested in community activities. The social aspect of community work occasions—threshing, butchering, quilting bees—were the most important to them, but they also understood the value of the sharing of work and the benefits of community concern and caring in times of misfortune.

The primitive medical care then available made home remedies and good home nursing much more important. The variety of dangerous diseases and the death rate of both adults and infants are the darker aspect of a generally rosy picture of childhood.

Everyone loves to tell tales of when they were young, and to mildly exaggerate either the hardships or the joys of those remembered times. Behind these half-legendary tales lie the real forces which molded the lives of the adults telling the stories.

And so it is with the narrators of this project. Their memories of their young years foreshadow what their adult lives were to be. A family-centered childhood produced women who are deeply interested in their own families. Either a respect for learning or a tendency to make education secondary to daily work loads are likely to be the outcome of parental attitudes of years gone by. A feeling of concern and a sharing of the joys and troubles of the neighborhood reflect attitudes formed in a time when sharing among community members was almost a necessity. Moral and religious values believed in and lived daily by parents produced children who believe in and practice the same precepts today. Children of hard-working parents, trained to work at an early age, still see great value in the work ethic in their adult years.

Childhood was fun, full of Ring-Around-The-Rosy and dolls; childhood was hard, full of milking and bringing in the wood for stoves. Childhood was lived in a rural setting, with wildflowers and creeks and lots of pets; childhood was skating on the sidewalks and listening to battery radios. Childhood was sad, with a sister crippled by polio or a mother dead from tuberculosis.

Childhood was many things, but our narrators share them all with us.

GROWING UP
IN MY HOME

*"I wish I could communicate my childhood memories.
I can feel now Grandfather Tower's rough warm hand
when he held mine as we walked down the dusty lane
to the pond. The quiet of "before Sunday School" time at the
house as Grandfather sat waiting for us to go to church,
often looking over his Sunday School lesson.*

*I can hear the sounds of the katy-dids,
the porch swing creaking, and the quiet voices of the
adults on the porch and in the yard,
when I was tucked in bed in a little cot by the window.*

*I wonder, in this day of noise and television and rush-about,
will children have these kinds of memories?"*

Sandra Tower Kean, Crawford County

Girls and their dolls. China head dolls were
treasured possessions of many little girls,
usually reserved for play at special times.
The less breakable rag dolls were taken
with the owners everywhere.
Photo taken in 1917.
Submitted by Steuben County

THE FAMILY
MEMBERS

We had a large family. My grandfather lived with us. I have nine brothers and one sister. I was the seventh child.

I learned to work hard, but we had a lot of fun doing the work we had to do. Back in that time every family had to work hard. Perhaps we didn't have clothes like other people. At that time maybe it was important, but as we grew older we had memories that outlaid that.

Libby McKinney, 54, Bartholomew County

We certainly didn't have the things the children have nowadays. We made our own entertainment. We learned early to help Mother and Dad to do the chores and work in the garden. We helped all ways that we could. We worked together. It wasn't one run here, one run there; we were a unit. We stayed together. The kids didn't run off to town themselves like they did later. There was no way. We just had a horse and buggy and carriage.

Alma Knecht, 78, Wabash County

In our neighborhood there was so many—there was about 20 kids, and the biggest part of them was relation, because that was the Rohrback section all around there. The brothers all had farms and then there were the aunts and their husbands and they had farms, too. So it was just a cousin neighborhood, with a few other neighbor kids.

Those days you had a lot of kids, you know, the more the merrier.

Masa Scheerer, 82, Huntington County

My dad's cousins used to come from Gary, and they stayed two weeks, and we'd have a whole line of kids on the floor.

It was summer and they could sleep on the floor.

There wasn't enough beds for everybody. One time we turned the beds crosswise and we slept crosswise on the beds. That way you [could] put four or five kids in a bed, instead of two or three. According to their size.

Edna Winter, 74, Pulaski County

We used to go down to Grandma and Grandpa's on a Sunday. If one of the brothers and sisters came, Grandma got on the telephone and invited all the other children and their families to come in. Sometimes we would be almost ready to sit down to our Sunday dinner, and the telephone would ring. "Well, Siren's just drove in; why don't you come down and have dinner with us?"

I don't know how she took it, because there must have been 25 grandchildren there. The girls went upstairs and the boys went to the barn. I had an aunt who was only three years older than I was, and the girls always went to her bedroom. It was boring to me, because those girls were enough older than I that they talked about their boyfriends and their new clothes . . . and I wasn't much interested in that.

The big thing down at Grandma's was to make candy. She would let us make butterscotch candy or chocolate fudge. She had a recipe for each and she would turn us loose in the kitchen to make candy. Can you imagine a grandmother turning kids loose in the kitchen? But she did! And she trusted us.

Grandma Bonnell had ten children and seemed to enjoy every one of them, along with the grandchildren and the great-grandchildren.

My Grandpa Penny loved kids, too. He used to whittle things for us. He'd made a whistle, but we'd have to stay outside to blow it, because it bothered Grandma Penny. And he showed us how to whistle with a blade of grass. He used to take us on walks through the grove and he told us about different kinds of trees and told how you could tell directions by the side the moss was on.

Mildred Weaver, 64, Pulaski County

Grandpa and Grandma lived up on the hill, about a quarter of a mile from our house. We could see their front porch from our house. We went up a lot and visited them.

Grandpa, in the wintertime, had on brown corduroy overalls and he had chin whiskers and a moustache all over his face. He was about five foot two inches, and weighed about 140 pounds. Grandma weighed a little more than that, and her garb was a brown checkered apron and a [sun] bonnet in the summertime. I remember them that way.

We would go up there and help them eat up the jelly that had been there long enough to form a crust on top.

I think the folks had a hard time keeping us from going up there all the time.

Archie Burnett, 81, Morgan County

I used to enjoy going down to Grandma's, especially if I could stay all night with them. I'd go with them while they did up their chores in the evening. We'd all go around and get the chores all done up. Frank would bring in a nice log to put on the fireplace and then, while Grandma fixed us a nice meal, I'd sit on Grandpa's lap before the fireplace and we'd watch the fire. It was the only light that was in the room.

Ethel Downen, 95, Montgomery County

I milked cows and put up hay in the summertime and I shocked wheat in the fields with my grandfather. He and I were very close. They said when I was growing up that you could always see a shadow behind Mr. Miller—there I would be, coming right along with him.

Elizabeth Elbrecht, 60, Dearborn County

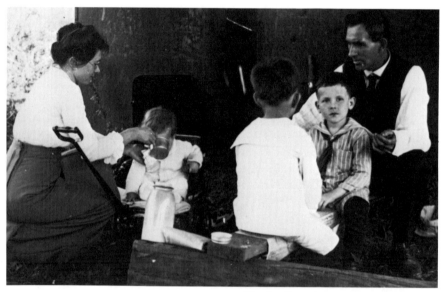

The family unit contained a loving husband and wife with a growing family.
Submitted by Whitley County,
L. M. Huffman, photographer

I was always so close to my Grandma Brinley. She died the year I married, in 1934, and it really affected me, because it was years before I quit dreaming about her. She was always that close to me.

Catherine Summers, 67, Harrison County

I don't know how my mother did all the things she did. There was all our family, which was six, and there was my grandmother, my uncle, and we almost always had one hired man, and sometimes two. All this with no electricity, washed the hard way—and we always had a white tablecloth on the table. She made all of the clothes for three girls. I never had a bought coat until I was 16. She always had a lot of company. She had a couple of old-maid cousins that came and just sat half the summer and didn't turn their hand to do anything. She was a little woman, and not too well. She was a marvelous cook. She had to have a system!!

Margaret Gibson, 87, Cass County

It took me all day to wash when I was first married, but can you imagine my mother washing sheets from nine beds, rubbing them by hand, then boiling them, and then doing all the equivalent that went along with that [for a big family]? Cooking meals, looking after a family. It was really something.

She would can around 1,000 quarts of fruit and vegetables a year. Besides that, my father put around 25 bushels of potatoes in the basement, and besides that they buried cabbage and apples and other root vegetables in a pit outdoors that was lined with straw so they would hold good until next spring. They brought cabbage in by the wagon-box load, too, not just a few heads. They raised cabbage for their chickens, too.

Around Christmas they would butcher. She would fill up her empty fruit jars with beef and pork. Then in the spring we always had enough maple trees to can around 100 quarts of maple syrup.

She did this, sewed for seven of us, besides helping the neighbors sew. And if there was a new baby in the neighborhood, she always went and stayed the first three or four days.

I always said she was 20 years younger than any daughter she had. The time she broke her wrist, she was carrying an armload of wood. She would run from the barn to the house with that load of wood.

Bernice Esch, 70, Lagrange County

Did you have a role model that you looked up to as you were growing up?

Well, I would have to say Mom. I always looked to her for advice and to me, really, she's my best friend and we can still talk about most anything. Really, she's my ideal.

Rosemary Flamion, 25, Perry County

My father used to like to play jokes on people. We had an upstairs window at the back of the house just above the door below. We kids took a bucket of water up there and set it on the window and put a string on it, so when you opened the door, it would tip the bucket (chuckles). He [father] always took a little nap after dinner, so we went out to the woodshed and watched (laughing). And he came out and it got him and he started after my brother, but he couldn't catch him (laughing). So then he'd get tickled and he's start laughing, but we

thought maybe, to begin with, he was going to thrash us (laughing).
So that was one of the funny things that happened.
Alvah Watson, 97, Allen County

My brother's entrance into my life when I was five was probably
when my world shook. He was a darling little boy who was really a
wanted baby, but I had to learn to live with this new baby around.
None of my friends had new babies—all of them had older brothers
and sisters. So adjustments did transpire in that time.
Jean Brechbill, 65, DeKalb County

I always kept looking for a stork to bring me a baby sister. And
when I was four, I got this baby sister. I sat in my little rocking chair,
all ready for the baby. They put her in my arms and she bawled.
Phyllis Frank, 79, DeKalb County

My fun and friends mainly were with my brothers and sister. We
had our share of fights, but it also helped to draw us very close
together. We had a lot of wide open space out in the country, and so we
did a lot of hiking and berry picking and had a lot of fun in that way.
We played a lot of ball, did lots of bike riding, but it was mainly with
family, rather than with friends.
Sarah Whitham, 40, Dearborn County

Were your mother and daddy strict?
Yes, they were. My father was strict. One time I went to the table
when I was in high school and I had a book in my lap. When we said
grace I was reading the book. He knew it. He told me to get down
from the table and he took my book. I never got it back.
Pearl Gordon, 94, Wells County

When we were at the table, we had to be orderly. And sometimes the
two brothers and I would get tickled at something, and our dad would
just say to us in a kind way, "Now, if you can't behave, leave the
table." Well, sometimes we'd leave the table or sometimes we would
quiet down.
Vida Mundy, 89, Lawrence County

When my father got up, he came to the stair door and he thumped
on the step and that meant everybody up—from the oldest to the tini-
est. And we all ate together. No stringing in for meals. That many kids,
you'd never get done.
Edna Winter, 74, Pulaski County

My dad was pretty close on all of us. We didn't get to go like other girls, but lots of times we done it anyway. One time we threw our clothes out the upstairs window, Grace and I, then we went down and went out and dressed and hitched up the horses and went to town. We didn't have anything in particular to go for, but we just wanted to go to town.

Mary Shields, 96, Blackford County

There was positively no drinking around our house. Father was very much against that. He told about how so many men would drink and leave their families without food and all, and he was very much against it.

Ruth Dane, 81, Madison County

Was dancing taboo?
Yes, and card playing as well. My brother—I don't know where he got a pack of cards but he did—and we kept it hidden in the organ where there was a place for the music. We kept the cards hidden there. So when they [parents] were gone once in a while, we would play cards. But that was taboo also.

Pearl Hiland, 96, Fulton County

Did you get punished?
No, talked to. It would have been better to have a spanking than to have my father talk to us. He never did spank, but he sure could talk. He would get you on his knee and he was so kind and loving. He could make you feel worse than if he had whipped you. Many times I would rather that he would, but he didn't.

Audrey Blackburn, 86, Posey County

As best I recall, never once did Edna Tower or Mommie Tower *ever* raise their voices or scold any of us kids, and God knows we probably needed it. To me that is the most remarkable self-control imaginable.

Nita Rausch, Crawford County

Was your mother the stronger disciplinarian than your father?
Yes, I'd say that she was. Now I don't mean that we had a hard home, I don't mean that at all. But Mother was very firm, and I knew better than to argue with her. I also knew that whatever my dad told me, it was that way, and I had better agree to it.
Don't you think that was basically the way all homes were—that the parents had a firm hand?

And you didn't dislike them for it. There was a lot more respect for authority.

Ruth Dye, 75, Martin County

And our father was very insistent that we eat bread. We didn't want to eat bread—I don't know why, but we didn't. He insisted; he called it the staff of life. So we sometimes stuck part of our slices under our plate so he wouldn't know we hadn't eaten them. Of course, (laughs) Mother would find it.

And the same way with fat meat. I could not eat fat meat, and I'd always put it under my plate, around where Mother and Father couldn't see it. I guess I thought they never would find it.

Many times Mother would get so disgusted with us that she'd go out to the cherry tree or the peach tree and get a little switch and switch us around the legs.

The whole family enjoys an inexpensive
treat of homegrown watermelon.
Submitted by an Extension Homemaker

In our house we had one room that both doors locked on the inside, so you could lock yourself in. So, I don't know what we had done, but Mother was going to switch us, and she went out to the cherry tree to get a switch.

We went into this room and locked both doors, and was going to live there all the rest of our lives. When she come in, of course, she saw we were in this room. She didn't say anything, just went on about her work.

She went out after a bucket of water. You always had to carry water from the well in those days. So my sister slipped out to the cupboard to get us something to eat. We were always piecing. She got something and brought it back in to us.

And so then, as was usual with her, after she had done something, then I had to do it the next time. So, next time Mother went out— probably she went purposely, discovering we had been into the cupboard—and it was my turn to go to the cupboard. Lennie insisted that I should go. So I went in the kitchen, and Mother stepped in just about the time I got to the cupboard.

I started back to the bedroom where we were locked in and I said, "Open the door quick, open the door quick." So Lennie opened the crack of the door and I slipped through, but Mother got her foot in the door.

So you can guess what happened (laughing). We got switched, not only for what we'd done, but also for running away from her.

But those were childhood days and we had a lot of fun. We didn't know that we didn't have a lot of things that other people had, but we enjoyed our childhood and our fellowship with one another very much, and loved our parents dearly.

Erma Agnew, 88, Decatur County

THE FAMILY HOUSE

Our dining room table was oval and long enough to seat twelve easily, which it did three times a day for several years. Quite often there were several others visiting; aunts, uncles, cousins, friends, and men who worked on the farm who joined us at this table for a meal.

We were taught by Mother the proper way to set the table and one of us always had the job for every meal. The table was always covered—an oilcloth for every day and a lace or white tablecloth for Sundays and special occasions.

Meals were never started until everyone was seated and Father had returned thanks.

Meals were just a beginning for our dining room table. Immediately after breakfast dishes were cleared, school lunches were started. This was Dorothy's job for years, and moved down the line as we grew up. It was an assembly line procedure, ending up with a line of lunches ready to be grabbed up as we flew out the door to school. Lots of days Mother would fry chicken in the morning so that each of us could take it for lunch that day. We had fruit, usually an apple, every day.

In the evening, as soon as the supper dishes were cleared up, it was homework time at the table. A good [kerosene] light was placed in the center of the table and we all gathered around. We soon learned not to procrastinate on our homework, as we were not allowed to stay up past bedtime on a school night no matter what.

During the 1937 flood, Dr. Deen and the county nurse set up their supplies on our dining room table and gave typhoid shots to many of the flood victims.

Wintertime was also comfort-making time. Mother made a few new ones every year. After she had the [comfort tops] sewed, she spread them over the table [together with the filling] and all the available girls in the family gathered around the table and helped tack. I'm sure Mother ended up doing a big part of the job herself, since she was so quick with her hands, but we all did learn something from the job.

Last, but not least, the dining room table was used for fun. Games, jigsaw puzzles, coloring, drawing, writing, scrapbooks and paper dolls—just to name a few—were among the many activities completed at the dining room table.

Margaret Booth, Crawford County

And the bedrooms weren't heated. Did you get pretty cold?
Oh, yes! Sometimes we'd find snow in the house in the morning. We had a summer kitchen my father built. In the summertime they would move into that little house [to cook]. And maybe we'd sleep out there until it got real cold. Sometimes you'd wake up in the morning and find snow on the floor that blew in under the door.

Mother always had plenty of covers. We didn't want for getting cold—we could keep warm. The main thing was getting up in the morning. You know, boy, that was awful!

Alvah Watson, 97, Allen County

As a child, I remember, we would come downstairs. We slept upstairs without any heat. And while they were getting the fires stoked up over the house early in the morning, we came into the kitchen. We had a combination wood stove and cooking stove. She would shut all the doors and fire up the cookstove in the kitchen, and we'd stay there until the rest of the house was warm enough to get out into. That's something we don't know about these days.

And we heated water on that cookstove and we had baby pigs

behind the stove when they were too little or had to be taken away from their mothers for some reason.

Alene McKinley, 47, White County

What was [your mother's] kitchen like?

It was quite a long, narrow kitchen and she had a table at one end where they would eat breakfast. The other end was the stove, and the work table.

Something that was unusual for that time, they had a sink in their kitchen. They had a pitcher pump and they had a cistern, and they could pump water from the cistern right into the kitchen. Of course, it wasn't heated. It was just cold water, but they did have that water in the kitchen.

And she heated the water in her cookstove?

Oh, yes, she had a big reservoir on the range, where she heated the water.

And had the warming ovens above?

Yes, I can remember making big batches of bread and she would put it in the dishpan to raise, just a great big, big lump of dough (laughs). Well, she would have eight loaves of bread at a time, you know—big loaves of bread. Because there was a big family, and they always had a hired man.

Anna Martin, 80, White County

We had a base burner in our living room, and [in the kitchen] we had a wood stove, a range to cook on. I had to carry in wood and coal. I had to pump the water and bring it in.

Didn't have a faucet?

No, we didn't have a faucet and we didn't have no rest room in the house.

Helen Shockey, 80, Grant County

What kind of bathing facilities did you have?

Washtub.

In the kitchen?

Yes, by the fire in the wintertime; in the summertime we would put the tubs outside and the sun would heat them, then we would bathe out there after dark. We didn't have any facilities where we could bathe.

Bernice Esch, 70, Lagrange County

What a difference water in the house made. When we were home, the washpan was our bathtub. I remember Dad put the washpan on the chair and put our heads over it and scrubbed our heads. It was wonderful to have water and be able to bathe every day and wash your clothes often. Why, you wash your clothes every day now; you sure didn't change clothes that often back then.

And, oh, to fix your vegetables in the sink and let the water run, when in the old days you had it in a pan and you didn't throw that water out for every little radish or carrot.

You lived in town. Did you have outhouses?

Oh, yes, we had outhouses and didn't like them at all. We had the outhouse and Dad did have a little cement walk out there. All the neighbors had them, too.

I'll never forget the week that we moved into this house. It was the last week in January. There was a room for the bathroom, but no plumbing in it. That first week we all got terribly sick, we had intestinal flu. The man was working to put the bath fixtures in, but we were so sick. Well, that was a bad week!

Frances Bennett, 63, Montgomery County

For light we had kerosene lanterns and kerosene lamps. The lamps were all over the house. And finally we was thrilled to pieces when we got a gasoline lamp, because it just looked like the whole house was lighter than with the coal oil lamp.

And we milked with a [kerosene] lantern all the time. Dad got up early and went to bed early.

Ruth Grover, 79, Wells County

As a child we didn't have electricity. We had a battery system that generated enough power that we could have lights and a radio, but that was about all. In the summertime we had a kerosene range and in the wintertime we had a wood stove and carried in wood and carried out ashes.

Luella Abell, 64, Jackson County

How did you keep your milk cold, and how did you preserve your food?

We had basements, cellars at that time, and they were cool. We kept vegetables, potatoes and apples down there nearly all winter. And we had a "hanging" shelf and on this shelf we would put our butter and milk, and it was kept cool [in the cellar].

I remember when we got our first icebox. I remember when they used to cut ice from Shipshewana Lake and bring it to town. We had a big icehouse uptown. They'd pack the ice in sawdust in the wintertime and in the summertime they'd take it out of the icehouse and wash off the sawdust and then sell it to the town people for their iceboxes. [Later] we had an iceman that used to come around with ice.

We had to empty the water pan underneath [the icebox] where the ice melted.

Bernice Esch, 70, Lagrange County

We had an upground cellar. You called it upground because the dirt was mounded up around it. It had a roof on it and ventilators, but you walked down into it. It had steep steps down.

It kept things at a nice even temperature. In the winter we would store potatoes and apples and they kept wonderful down there. And all our canned fruit was down there.

Mother kept a top shelf in there where she kept her pies and cakes. And she would never bake under two cakes at a time, and maybe three or four pies at a time.

Ruth Grover, 79, Wells County

CHORES

What about leisure time activities when you were young?

Well, we didn't have much leisure time, when I was young. I was working all the time. Today they have too much leisure time. Too much leisure time on their hands and not enough to do. I think the children would be better off if they had more responsibilities.

Opal Becker, 78, Noble County

Farmers never worried about calories. Did you hear talk about calories?

Oh, no. We never worried about calories. Calories is something new—since Home Ec. (laughs). We worked. We didn't have to worry about calories. We worked. Everybody worked. Clear down to the little ones. Soon as they could understand, they had their chores. There was wood to carry in. There was water to pump. My dad usually had 40 or 50 head of cattle and that water was all pumped by hand. Milking was all done by hand. The wood all had to be cut and carried in. We worked.

Edna Winter, 74, Pulaski County

GENERAL CHORES

Every morning we had to get up and milk our cow, wash the dishes, cook breakfast, before we went to school. In the summertime we were out in the hayfield, cornfield, garden, shocked wheat. We worked in all of it.

Rosalia Mehringer, 79, Dubois County

There was a big family of us, we had fifteen children in our family, with three sets of twins. We'd get up about six in the morning to get our work done. The boys had to milk and feed the pigs and all that before school.

Then when we'd get in of an evening, we always knew what chores we had to do. Some got the water in for the night, some got the coal and the wood, some to the barn to milk.

The first thing was to change our dresses so we'd have them nice and clean for the next day.

You wore the same dress the next day?

Practically all week, because my mother washed on a board, so we had to be careful with our dress. Sometimes we didn't wear it a week, but we did if it was clean enough.

But we had our chores cut out for us at home, and everybody went right to their chores and got them all done. Then, after supper of a night, we all got our lessons.

Mary Sheeks, 73, Lawrence County

When we came home from school, the first thing was "Where's Mom?" Then after you had seen Mom, "You children better get your clothes changed. It's getting dark and you have to get your chores done."

There was ashes to carry out and coal to bring in. You usually need two or three coal buckets for that one hard coal burner [stove].

Alma Knecht, 78, Wabash County

Another chore that went with the cookstove—Dad always cut the wood and did the splitting himself, didn't want to be bothered—but then we'd go back there and cord the wood and leave it there all summer. Just before school started, [we would] bring it into the woodshed and stack it up. There would be several ricks, maybe 10 ricks for the cookstove, and then several ricks outside for the heating stove. We kept one stove going all the time, and sometimes two. The parlor [stove] was lit up once in a while.

Archie Burnett, 81, Morgan County

We had an enclosed back porch and we'd have to pile the wood in there and the buckets of coal and everything. The boys would always get that in at night for the heater, so we would have plenty of fuel and it would be dry.

I remember on that back porch there was a table painted white with a crock setting on top of it, full of water for our drinking water, with a dipper in it. In the wintertime it was really cold when you would go out there to get a drink.

Anna Martin, 80, White County

The first chore we had as a youngster was to carry in water and keep the reservoir [on the cookstove] full of water.

[Speaking] of the water bucket reminds me of another chore. Our well water was so "hard." That means it contained excessive amounts of orangish brown clay mineral particles. It would settle in the long-handled granite water dipper and on the insides and bottom of the granite water bucket. I didn't think it looked clean, but I disliked the times I had to take Dutch Cleanser and scour them white again.

Lorene Shirk, 65, Decatur County

OUTDOOR CHORES

Dad never let Lucille [sister] and I work at the barn. We never went to the field to work and we never milked. We did help with the chickens. But Dad always said (of course he had the two older boys to help him), but he always said, "Your place is to help your mother, and I don't want you out around here, with the stock."

Anna Martin, 80, White County

We had a lot of chores. We had to help with the milking and feeding chickens. I helped in the garden.

But my father was one of those—he didn't want the women working out in the fields. He was very strict about that. We would beg to work. I liked to get out with the horses, but he wouldn't let me.

Dora Giggy, 79, Lagrange County

I grew up on the farm and there was a big family of us, but there wasn't near as many boys as there was girls, so the girls had to work in the fields, too. I have helped to plant corn and hoe corn and most everything.

Maggie Owen, 95, Whitley County

My dad had no boys and he always called me Tommy. The other three girls worked in the kitchen and around there, but I always helped feed the horses and hogs and do things like that. Everything he did, like plant clover seed, I'd help him do it. And he called me Tommy.

Mara Meyer, 84, Knox County

One of the fondest memories I have is a spring morning walking out our back door and seeing my dad hitching up the horses to get ready to plow and to plant corn. I can remember beautiful spring days and we had an orchard behind our house and it would be in bloom. Just sparkling days. And to go out and see the horses being hitched up—it is one of my best memories.

Rebecca Stewart, 35, Franklin County

I was put to weeding onions and picking pickles and stuff like that, because I believe she thought that the devil finds some mischief still for idle hands to do.

Anna Surfus, 85, DeKalb County

My father was a market gardener. He rented 13 acres in the north-west part of the city. If you've ever been a childhood gardener, you learned how to work. He had seven children; no wonder he could be a gardener. They could all handle hoes and do a great deal of work in the garden. We even delivered the vegetables on a couple of bicycles we had.

Camille Hey, 89, Shelby County

In about 1917 we lived at DeMotte and my dad planted a lot of garden. My job was to weed and cultivate and then I'd go with him to take the vegetables to Gary or different places, and we'd sell them.

Ann Elijah, 69, Newton County

I was the oldest girl in a family of 10, so I had many, many chores. My father was a melon farmer, so the first day school was out, we started to plant watermelons. I worked right in the field with my father and brothers and my sister.

We had semi trucks that came to our farm from out of state every year. The day before [they came] my dad would go out in the melon patch and he would cut them and I would help him stack them in rows. Then the day the semi came, I would be up in the back of the truck and my father on the ground. He would pitch the melons to me and I would load the truck!

Luella Abel, 63, Jackson County

All of us worked in the fields. We raised onions by the train carload, not by the handful. All of us worked in the fields in the summertime; Mother, all of us girls, and all the boys that were at home worked in the fields.

It wasn't hardly fair—the men would come to the house at noon; they would feed the stock and then they would sit down while Mother and us girls had to get the lunch ready. The men could eat, sit down, and rest again while we cleared up. There wasn't any rest for us—we just had to go back to the field. Same way in the evening. When we would get through in the evening, Dad and the boys got their chores

Dorothy Arnholt enjoyed working
in the fields, helping her father with the
farm chores, in the 1930s.
Submitted by Bartholomew County

done and they could quit. But our work went on and on, because we had to get ready for the next day.

What did you do when you went to the onion fields?

Oh, (sighs), crawled on your hands and knees and weeded the onions. Your onions are planted about a foot apart in rows. They had to be absolutely kept clean. They were raised on muck and that is HOT. It would be down in the hollow, and breezes were few and the sun was hot.

They would go down through them with what we called a wheel-hoe to cultivate them. Then we had to go through and hand weed every row.

One summer it was 90° in the shade and we worked down there, and all the neighbor kids were going swimming and having such fun. And here we were, weeding onions! That fall the onions weren't worth anything, so my father stored them. He never could sell them and the next spring he hauled them out to the field and plowed them under. Bushel after bushel after bushel of onions and plowed them under.

After all that work!

We might as well have gone swimming, too!

Bernice Esch, 70, Lagrange County

My father was a farmer and a mint raiser, which took a lot of help from the children. We did hand weeding. We usually got rewarded with something special at the end of the season. One thing that I remember specially is that we got a player piano for our work for one season.

Ellen McAfee, 68, Marshall County

The farm we lived on had rocks on it, and every year after the plowing was done and the cultivating and everything, rocks would work themselves up through the soil. We did spend quite a bit of time picking rocks off those fields, and that's a back-breaking job.

Floy Jacobus, 53, Gibson County

I remember Mother's sister telling this story on herself. One June, after the corn was coming through the ground, it was her job to take the hoe and more corn and replant it. She grew tired of this and hid the rest of the corn under a rock in the field. When the rains came, the corn sprouted and grew out from under the rock. Her father found the corn and she was punished.

Tom Tower, Crawford County

There were times when he [father] would have weeds to get out of corn. He would hitch a horse to an iron wheel and we would drive the horses through the corn to drag the ground to help smooth it out.

Did you set on the wheel, or did you set on the horse?

He fixed a platform on the wheel. We just drove the horse and set on the platform.

Thelma Nixon, 68, Union County

And sorghum cane—I had to help strip cane, and I sure hated that.

What do you mean by "strip cane?"

Well, strip the leaves all off of the stalks. And them leaves would cut you—it was an awful job.

Pearl Kinkaid, 79, Owen County

I used to shuck corn—we'd have to go out and shuck corn in the morning, before we went to school. We went out and helped our dad get a load of corn before we went to school, and that was terrible.

I had several brothers, and they all took a separate wagon and went and picked corn. So I wanted to do that, instead of going with one of them. I took my wagon and started out before daylight. I'll never forget that day. I was driving down the road and they were ahead of me and it was just light enough that you could see.

I thought there was something following me. It kind of scared me. We had to go a mile down the road and then back in the field and I watched that thing and watched it and it was getting a little bit lighter and finally, when I did make out what it was, it was another horse following away back. One of the old white horses, but it really had me a-goin'.

Bertha Pampel, 83, Benton County

I remember, after we got big enough, we had to mow the lawn. It was an old-time push mower, of course, and we had to go over it [lawn] the first time with a sickle and cut all the buckhorn down, and then we went over it with the old lawnmower. You wear out in a little bit, and you had to sort of change around and have somebody take your place while you got your breath.

Lennie Hern, 90, Decatur County

I always liked to help in the garden. It was my job to raise the flowers. Our garden was north of the house. We had quite a nice lawn and the garden joined with the lawn. I always had two rows of flowers between the lawn and the garden. And then at the west end there was a corner and I had that in flowers most of the time.

I remember when I wasn't very big yet, when Mother would make garden, I'd want a garden of my own. So she'd give me a little patch of ground, maybe five or six feet square, back of the old toilet, and that was my garden. I had a little hoe and she'd give me some seed and I'd plant them.

I remember one time I was going to have some morning glories, and I put some stakes in the ground and I planted my morning glories. They all came up and got to running up them stakes. But Dad saw them and said, "You got to get them out of there. I'm not going to have no morning glories." So I had to dig them out.

He considered them a type of weed then?

There were a weed, just common morning glories.

Anna Martin, 80, White County

If she [mother] would tell me to go outside and pull weeds or work outside, I loved the outdoors and I still do. Nothing that she could make me do outdoors made me mad. But if it came to something inside, I could always not hear her at all.

Eleanor Cheek, 61, Union County

So come time to pick strawberries, Uncle Joe Allison would send us word when to come. They had a big patch. You know how strawberries have a row; then there's straw; then there's another row. You'd crawl along there.

They'd give us a carrier that had six quart boxes in it. You were to fill these, but you weren't going to put in any green ones, and you weren't going to put in any that was spoiled. And we'd crawl along, and by noon I know, several days, I picked 20 gallons of berries. I got 5¢ a gallon.

Five cents a gallon? Real big pay!

Yes, and then I decided that I wanted to get me a hat to wear to Sunday School, because in those days everybody would wear hats. So Mother took me to town, and I got a little one—they called it a leghorn hat—had a wide rim to it, with little ribbons around the crown of it and streamers that hung down in the back. And I paid a dollar and a half. It took me three days to make enough to buy that hat.

Pearl McCall, 89, Daviess County

We would go out in the fall [and get walnuts]. It wasn't everybody that had a corn sheller, but we had a corn sheller. And the boys would come there with their walnuts [unhulled]. And we'd take the sheller out and they would run maybe a half bushel of walnuts [through the sheller]. And that would loose the shells, and they'd throw an ear of corn in, and then they'd put in more walnuts and more corn. [They'd] let the chickens scratch that and eat the corn. They'd come back in a few days and the corn would be gone and the walnuts would be all dried, and they'd sell them.

And hickory nuts, if you had the shell bark, we could get $1.00 a bushel [shelled], but if it was the bull nuts, you could only get about 60 cents. So that was what we looked forward to, to getting any money.

Alvah Watson, 97, Allen County

It was during the Depression and they were going to have Old Settlers' Day, which is a carnival type thing that came up to Columbia City once a year. In order to earn money, I would go out and gather potato bugs—to earn money to ride on things at Old Settlers' Day. I don't think many kids now days would get out and do that. 'Course, I had to gather an awful lot of potato bugs to get a penny, even (laughs). But it was fun.

LaVerda Shearer, 56, Whitley County

Barefoot time came in the spring after the ground had warmed. These feet would not see shoes again, except for going to church, until school started in the autumn.
Submitted by Knox County

We sold berries. We picked blackberries and brought them to Loogootee and sold them for 10¢ a gallon.

And I think last summer they sold for $4.00, at least.

Yes, but we sold them for 10¢ a gallon. But there was a lot of them.

My, you could go out in the morning and just pick enough to have a whole buggy full in the afternoon. But, my, that was a lot of work for 10¢.

And got lots of chiggers to go with them. Always took a bath and put fried meat grease on them, but we would pick all day and scratch all night. And Mom would get me down and look for ticks in my hair every time after we would go berrypicking, too.

Cleo Borders, 77, Martin County

My father had four lots on the edge of Kewanna and he had a pig pen there with a couple of pigs that he fattened up to butcher in the winter. There was a bucket set by the kitchen door where we put scraps and dish water and sour milk and everything into the bucket and put it in the barrel. Then we would get what was called "shorts," it was bran, the whole grain and not just the bran. We would stir that into it and it would sour.

Beer always reminded me of that slop barrel.

Pearl Hiland, 96, Fulton County

You had to break the ice out of the buckets and out of the troughs and feed the pigs, slop the hogs I should say. And we always went out and got old bread and stuff, and we had to break open all the packages and throw it out to them. We had to go out and try to turn the valves on for the troughs, and sometimes we couldn't budge them. And then, when they got out, chase them down the road!!

Ellen Doss, 34, Clark County

You didn't have running water?

We had running water. You pumped water in a bucket and then you run with it (laughter). We had an old-fashioned tank heater in the cement tanks and we burned coal in there. The heater set in the middle of that cement tank and it kept the ice soft enough so that the cattle could break it with their nose and get water.

Ruth Grover, 79, Wells County

We had calves every year and you had to teach them how to drink out of a bucket. You put your hand in their mouth, then you put it down in the milk, then gradually take it away and they'd put their nose down in the milk. They'd just suck it without realizing.

Grace Heinzman, 86, Hamilton County

Back then we had to herd our cows along the road. We had milk cows. Two neighbor girls and my oldest brother started herding [together]. The cow all of a sudden didn't give very much milk at night, so Dad was going to sell the cow.

We had to confess we were taking our tin cups with us and when we were herding her in the afternoon, the neighbors and me and my brother would drink the milk. So, in order to save the cow we had to tell what we were doing.

Pearl Sollars, 70, Tippecanoe County

I remember going to pick up the cows. We had a big pasture in a field a mile from home, and we'd go bring them home. We had a big cow we called Roan, and we'd jump on her back and ride her. Sometimes she'd get tired of having us on her, and there was a patch of trees there which she'd go under to switch off flies—and she'd go under it to try to switch us off (laughing).

Mara Meyer, 84, Knox County

I can remember going to the pasture fields to get the cows late in the afternoon. It was nice to walk down the lane on the nice cool grass late in the afternoon to bring the cows in.

Floy Jacobus, 53, Gibson County

I went to the barn every morning with my stepfather to feed. I helped milk. I had a little three-legged stool and I helped milk every morning. I had a wonderful stepfather and he never asked any of his other children to go to the barn, only just me. He could depend on me to get my old cow milked and then I'd help him shuck corn. They used to cut corn, haul it in the barn, put it in the loft and they you'd go up and throw just enough to feed the cows and horses. So many ears, three and four. I always liked to do that.

Mary Foltz, 93, Grant County

When we were at home, my father told us when we were seven years old we had to start milking cows. So on our 7th birthday, the next morning we took a milk bucket and started milking.

Ethel Meyer, 78, Ripley County

We milked cows and I used to—when Dad was working away from home—we'd think it was great if we could go get the cows in and have the milking done by the time he got home. Sometimes we made it and sometimes we didn't.

We learned to milk because he had an old gentle cow named Bessie.

And she didn't care if my brother milked on one side and I milked on the other. We'd milk in a tin cup, one on each side.

Mary Ruth Swarts, 66, Hancock County

You know, we don't milk now, but there isn't a day goes by that at five o'clock in the morning and five o'clock at night that I don't look at the clock and still think, "It's milking time."

Judi Merkel, 34, Adams County

One day we were on a hay rake, in the barnyard. Mother came to the door and she said, "I want you to stay right where you are. Now don't get off of that rake." We didn't know what she meant.

But here a dog come up out of the ditch. He was black and he was wobbling and he had slobbers stringing clear down in his face. Well, this was a mad dog. He was running free in the country, and they were trying to trace him down. He had got in that big open ditch and they didn't see him.

But when he got where we lived, he got up out of there and he come up and he went right down across our barnyard and went right on down into the schoolyard. Didn't look either way. And our mother was standing there on the porch; and there us kids was, all out there on the hay rake. It was panicky for her.

Mary Wolf, 88, Huntington County

The barn was our grandfather's pride and joy. It was built about 1905. I can remember the barn raising, the wide center driveway, the hay mows on either side, the doors tall enough to drive in a full load of hay—doors on rolling tracks, a system of ropes and pulleys and a hay fork for unloading.

But, best of all, from the middle of the highest roof rafters over the driveway was a rope swing with a wide board swing seat, securely fastened. We could, and did, swing the length of the driveway, high, high up, hour after hour, month after month, year after year, for two generations.

During the 1937 flood, the houses in Leavenworth were threatened and they were anchored down with ropes. The supply of rope was all used up. Dr. H. H. Deen's house was threatened. Poppie Tower cut down the hay-unloading ropes, cut down the swing ropes, and they were used to anchor down Dr. Deen's house to a big tree. It stood. Somehow the swing built for us kids and the eventual use of the rope sort of tells the story of Poppie's life.

Other memories of the barn: the wood pegs on which the harness hung; the post on which the string of sleigh bells hung; Old Betty and all her little colts; the sheep shed and the lambs; the smell of curing hay; the chug, chug of the steam engine at threshing time; the golden wheat as it came from the separator. Poppie's hands as he ran them through the plump kernels; the numberless cows I milked in this barn; the barn swallows' nests plastered to the wall of the horse stable; the barn cats lined up for a pan of warm milk that Poppie poured for them at each milking, on the theory that cats were better than mice. The golden wheat straw that bedded down the animals; the sound of the animals chewing their grain, fodder and hay while we milked; and, above all, the soft glow of the lantern light, just enough to keep me from feeling afraid of the dark.

Juanita Leech, Crawford County

We had geese. They used the goose grease and also the duck [grease] for a remedy. They made a salve out of it for your sore throat.

I remember Mother said you had to be careful when you pick the geese that you don't shut their wind off, when you turn their head down. But she said you had to be careful they don't bite you, too.

She would rather I'd pick the ducks than the geese, because they weren't so heavy and hard to handle.

She used to pick all those down feathers off and she would use them in pillows. We always had some geese around.

And another thing we had you don't see much any more was guineas. We used to have those, and if anything disturbed around the hen house at night, they would make that awful cackling noise. They never slept in the [hen] house, they always slept in the trees. The folks thought they would frighten away the animals that would come up around the hen house. We had so many wild animals like the skunk, the possum. Things like that would get in the hen house and take chickens. And bigger animals, fox and coon.

Alvah Watson, 97, Allen County

My mother sure raised a lot of chickens. Them days you didn't have incubators to hatch them; they had to hatch them under the old hens. Then Mother would have about 200 little chickens she would have hatched out and [she would] raise them for eating and keeping a few hens over for laying.

Masa Scheerer, 82, Huntington County

You hatched your eggs under an old hen. She would lay eggs so long, then she'd get to setting, so then you'd gather your eggs and set the eggs under her and watch them until they hatched.

If you wanted some early chickens, and your old hen wouldn't set, then you'd check with your neighbors and see if they had any hens setting. Many a time I've walked down the road to Maggie Bishop's and carried home a setting hen. She'd flop you on the legs and sometimes it would hurt.

Beulah Grinstead, 68, Hamilton County

Before we began buying baby chicks from the hatchery, Mother would set the hens on the eggs and raise her own. And then she had little metal coops with wire in front of them. Many times the crows would come and pick up the baby chicks when they were real tiny. And foxes would take chickens, grown chickens.

Thelma Nixon, 68, Union County

A little girl feeds her mother's
prize chickens.
J. C. Allen Collection

Mother raised chickens, and she would have an incubator in our parlor and she would hatch her chickens there. It was interesting to see them hatch out, come out of the shell. That was fun.

Phyllis Frank, 79, DeKalb County

One thing I loved to do was to gather in the eggs in the late afternoon. My mother always had a large number of Plymouth Rock hens. We had a special building we called the chicken house. There were straw nests there for them to lay their eggs in and there were planks for them to roost on at night.

When it was egg-gathering time I would take a basket and go out to the henhouse and take all of the eggs out of the nests and put them in the basket. There was usually a china nest egg in each nest that was left in the nest.

Ruth Snyder, 83, Marshall County

The part I didn't enjoy was reaching under an occasional old hen which had "gone to setting." That means she was ready to sit on a nest to hatch a batch of baby chicks. She was in no mood to have me steal her eggs, as she felt I was doing when I gathered eggs. If I was quick enough, I could reach under her and get an egg before she pecked me once or several times.

I would tell Mother, [and she] would put the "setting hen" into a coop for a few days to "break her" from wanting to "set." Then gathering eggs was an easy job again.

Lorene Shirk, 65, Decatur County

Another notorious thing was trying to evade my grandmother's old flopping rooster. When I would be away from the house for a long time, someone had to come to retrieve me. They quite often found me in the outside privy, with that rooster standing guard outside the door, just daring me to come out.

Mary White, 75, Hancock County

[We would] crawl under the old barn to get the eggs the hens laid there. I don't suppose you would use them at all, now, but we thought it was wonderful to find them. I don't know how long they had been there, but we took them in, and mother tried them out in water. If they sunk, she thought they were good and she used them.

Margaret Butler, 87, Steuben County

Did your mother raise hens?
We had eggs and chickens both for our own use and we sold them to the huckster. Ever so often they'd get past the laying stage and we'd get in the chicken house and help catch chickens.

Was this her money, then?
They always had a great big old pitcher up in the corner of the cabinet and if we needed a little bit of money, well, there it was. The egg money went there, and there used to be what they called the rag man came around and that money went in the pitcher, too.

Then when we went to town or to the grocery store or the fair, why we'd get to spend some of that money.

Edna Maddox, 71, Grant County

HOUSEHOLD CHORES

Did you have chores to do around the home?
Oh, yes. My mother always said run and do this. She never told us to walk, it was run and do it.
Margaret Garrison, 82, Wabash County

My life was hard. When I was five and a half years old, my mother married my stepfather and she had six children. I didied them and played with them, raised them up and helped with them when I got able to work.
Mary Foltz, 93, Grant County

My brother was eight years younger than me. I help her [mother] with my brother, took care of him, and watched him, seeing he didn't get in trouble.
Grace Elrod, 85, Jasper County

I had to look after the younger children. I had three brothers and the youngest was seven years younger than I.
So you had to take care of them and babysit them.
I remember rocking my baby brother and my mother tried to get supper the first year I started to school. I was reading and I asked her what the words meant. She took the book away and put it on top of the mantel, way up high, so I couldn't possibly read.
Mabel Bobbit, 88, Shelby County

What were your chores as a little girl?
Dusting, which I hate to do to this day.
Thelma Fox, 74, Shelby County

The thing I didn't like to do was make a bed. When we were children and after we were married, for a number of years, we always had a feather bed on top of our mattress. That feather bed would have to be beat up every day, so that you'd have a nice soft bed for the night. I never did like to do that. Now, of course, we have no feather beds, but I still don't like to make a bed.
Emma Baker, 78, Scott County

It was always our job to clean the house every Saturday. And my mother would always tear out something before she left for work—like the old buffet, she'd take all the dishes out. We were to have them washed and back in before she got back home. We would wait until just a few minutes before she came back home. Then we would work like crazy to get them washed and back in the cupboard.

Sarah Zeigler, 53, Adams County

We lived in a house with no running water. As a result, all our water had to be heated on a stove. This made such chores as washing clothes and rather simple household chores more difficult. My sister and I, one of our chores was the handwashing. We used a washboard, which is something I'm glad I don't have to use any more.

Sarah Whitham, 40, Dearborn County

My mother washed on a [wash] board and we had to carry the water down into the cellar. There was a drain there where we could empty the water. But we had to carry all the clothes and washing to the cellar and then bring it back upstairs, hang it on lines out in the yard, and it took all day long to hang up the washing.

Susie Burkhart, 67, Jackson County

What about your laundry facilities, can you describe them?

When I was little our washing machine was one that we had to turn the handle. It was on the back porch and my brother and I had to take turns. We counted how many turns [of the handle] we made. You had to keep a good count.

What about ironing? Did you have Tuesday ironing at your house?

Yes, it certainly was. Monday was wash day and Tuesday was ironing day. The only time I would iron would be in the summertime because I would be in school. Those were the irons that you had to heat on the stove.

Dora Giggy, 79, Lagrange County

I learned to sew by the time I was 11. I did my own sewing. Then I was able to make my own clothes. My sister did the same thing.

Birdena Day, 62, Wells County

I sewed ever since I could hold a needle, I guess. I made a dress before I started to school. Mother helped me. And I pieced a quilt when I was five years old. She cut me out big blocks about nine inches square. She'd pin two blocks together and make a pencil mark across where I was to put the stitches. And she gave me some colored thread, because I always thought that was prettier. And I would sew them blocks together. Then she finished it up. I had that quilt for a long time.

And I sewed for my dolls. I made all kinds of things for my dolls.
   Anna Martin, 80, White County

We were in a big old farmhouse that had a huge kitchen. My mother often would stretch the table out for [hired] hands. Hay hands and silo-filling hands. We had company Sunday after Sunday. She baked pies like you wouldn't believe. Anywhere from six to 13 pies at a time.
   I helped her when I got old enough. I packed the school lunches, I washed dishes. I did lots of things.
   I was so small I had to stand on a box and I asked her if she'd let me bake the cake this time. So I stood on the box and she got it down to the place where you add the flour. She said, "I think you can finish all right. I'm going to make the beds." When she came back, I had her cake mixed up like a loaf of bread—it was really stiff. You could knead it.
   Beulah Grinstead, 68, Hamilton County

Mother would go outside to do her work and she'd say, "Now, Della, you see to it that you bake this morning." But you know it was fun. I baked bread and cakes and pies and everything from when I was a little one. I learned to do it and I enjoyed doing it.
   Della Ackerman, 77, Noble County

I had a sister who liked outdoor work better, so I did the cooking and worked inside. I could bake better bread when I was 12 years old than I can now. I always said it was cornbread and fried potatoes every night, because that is what I liked and the rest of them were just glad to eat.
   Thelma Reedy, 80, Jay County

When I was a girl at home, I worked just like all little girls work. I done farm work and I helped to cook. I helped my mother in many ways. She would make a shoo-fly and I would try and kill the flies and shoo them out of the summer house where we lived in the summertime.
   Clara Nichols, 79, Wabash County

No doubt you were busy in the kitchen as you got older.
   Oh, yes. Mother and I always canned 400 to 500 quarts of things every summer. We didn't have freezers then and it was always our aim to get 100 quarts of tomatoes and 100 quarts of [green] beans canned to serve during the winter.
   Elizabeth Elbrecht, 60, Dearborn County

I remember how we had to kill the chickens. My mother had to go out and catch her chicken first, and chop its head off. It was my job, after we dipped it up and down in a big bucket of boiling water, to

Gathering in the eggs,
a farm girl's chore every evening.
J. C. Allen Collection

help pull all the feathers out. I can remember she always built a little fire outside and then held the chicken over it and singed all the rest of the little hairs and the pinfeathers off.

Now we just go to the grocery store and buy our chicken already cut up.

Norma Trent, 45, Dubois County

My grandmother allowed me to cut up my first chicken and to bake my first batch of bread. I did most of the breadbaking at home, even before I went to school in the morning. I mixed up the bread, because I was taller and stronger than my sisters, so it was up to me to do that. It doesn't seem to me today that it takes that much strength to mix bread. Of course, we made great big batches. Mother baked eight loaves at a time and we baked bread about twice a week.

Neva Schlatter, 79, Pulaski County

Mainly I cooked. Peeling stacks of potatoes, seemed like that was all I ever got done. With such a large family it took a lot of potatoes. The men had to have something that really filled them up.

Libby McKinney, 54, Bartholomew County

My mom taught me to cook real, real young. I think most farm women did that then. So it was no problem for me at the age of eight or nine to go into the kitchen and prepare a meal—I know I really liked to fry chicken.

My mom became quite ill and was taken to the hospital. To me it seemed like she was there forever. I had to come home after school to an empty house, because my dad wasn't home from work yet. So that was a sad time.

But I knew I had to have supper ready when Daddy got home. So I can remember having fried chicken and gravy and fried chicken and gravy. Once in a while pork—ham and fried potatoes and gravy. Seems like every meal consisted of gravy, but my dad liked gravy real well.

Mary Ann Hoskins, 49, Grant County

What is your most disliked aspect of homemaking?

WASHING DISHES! We always had so many people staying with us that it was like washing dishes for threshers every meal! That gets to be most exasperating!

You always had to carry your water and heat your water.

And wash in dishpans; we didn't have a sink. I always had to wash the dishes, because I was the oldest of the second family: my mother had four children, then there was a long space, then she had four more.

I was the oldest of the last four. So I had to wash the dishes, and my younger sisters had to dry. Stood on boxes to reach the dishpans, if you please, when we started.

Did you and your sisters have some spats during dishwashing?

Lots of them! I didn't have any choice, but generally the spats were between my younger sisters, as to who would dry what (laughing).

Bernice Esch, 70, Lagrange County

What were your facilities for washing dishes? Did you have running water in your house?

No, there wasn't anybody in town that had running water when I was little. We had a pump. The pump for the drinking water was outside, but we did have a pump on the inside that was connected with a cistern.

The hot water was fastened on the stove in a reservoir and that's where we had the hot water, on the little cookstove.

Bernice Hirst, 87, Lagrange County

We had to do our dishes before we could go to school. It didn't make any difference how late it was, Mother said, "You do the dishes first." If we had to run all the way to school, we ran all the way to school. It made us do it perfect the next day.

Della Ackermann, 77, Noble County

I always had to dry the dishes and when I dried the dishes I always sang. My mother would get so tired of hearing me sing the same song. I would sing "Up on the housetop, click, click, click. Down through the chimney with good St. Nick," everytime I dried dishes.

Beulah Mardis, 76, Johnson County

She would want me to wash the dishes, but I found out the best way to get out of that was to go in and practice my music. I played the piano, and I would always say, "Well, it's time for me to practice, and after I practice, I'll wash the dishes." Then I would practice a long time and she usually would have them done.

Gaby Moon, 69, Clay County

We had seven cows and us kids used to make a fuss over them. We would curry them like Dad would the horses. Us kids we could all milk, and we'd help out. It was always strain the milk and the next day we'd skim off the cream. In them days they didn't come around and gather up the cream or anything. We had to churn butter, then Mother would keep that real nice and cool and then they would take it to town on Saturday and sell butter for 12¢ a pound. Can you imagine that?

Beulah Grinstead, 68, Hamilton County

And what did you do with the milk?

We separated it, and sold cream.

Was this your job?

No, I never ran the separator too much. I was a very skinny young person and I didn't have the wind. My dad ran the separator. I guess I grew up that that was a man's job. But I've made many a trip to town with the cream. You had no refrigeration, so it had to go two and three times a week. You just had your basement for cooling. So in summertime it could sour pretty easily.

Tell me what you made out of cream.
We made butter out of cream. And we took the skim milk and made cottage cheese. The bulk of it we poured to the pigs after we got the cream out of it. It made nice fat pigs.

What did you think about oleo, back then? Did you ever eat it?
Yes, I can remember when we bought white oleo. And it came with a little pill of coloring pressed into the oleo. And you let the oleo set at room temperature and then you broke that little capsule and with the butter paddle you worked the color into the oleo. And you had to be pretty good, or it was striped. It was a very hard thing to work color into oleo.

Why didn't they color it?
It all came white. I don't remember when colored oleo came in. Sometimes it wouldn't be the right season and we wouldn't have milk to get our cream and butter and we would buy oleo. Run to the store and get it. But it all came white.
Edna Winter, 74, Pulaski County

Another chore I helped with was the churning. We had a dash churn at first. It was a wooden container, tall but not very big around, with a lid on it and there was a hole in the middle of the lid. A handle, something like a broom handle, went through the hole and stuck up above the churn about two feet. The other end went to the bottom of the churn and had a dash on it—two crosspieces of wood.

The sour cream was put in the churn, and I would take hold of the handle and make it go up and down, up and down, until the butter "came."

Then my mother would take a wood paddle and take the butter out of the churn and put it in a large wooden bowl. Then she would work it with the paddle.

Later, we had what was called a barrel churn. It was shaped like a barrel, only much smaller. It was set lengthwise in a frame with a handle at one end. Turning the handle made the barrel go round and round, so that eventually the butter would "come," just as in the dash churn. I think it was much easier to use. My arms didn't get quite so tired.
Ruth Snyder, 83, Marshall County

We did the churning, We had a stone churn at one time, with a dasher. You just up and down, up and down. In later days we had a glass [churn] that had a crank in it.

Vida Mundy, 89, Lawrence County

My mother was a pretty good hand to keep us busy all the time. It was her idea that she didn't want us to grow up lazy, and I can see where it was really quite important. When you have that training, you feel you have responsibility. When you see something that needs to be done, I think you'll come nearer doing it, than if you had never been trained to go ahead and do.

It's just entirely different. If they don't have something to go to now, they don't know what to do with theirselves. They're climbing the walls. Back when I grew up, all these little things that you had to do were regular chores that you did all the time. You grew up with some responsibility and something to occupy your time.

Beulah Rawlings, 76, Hamilton County

Children had chores they were responsible for each day. Now children have nothing they have to do, and they get so bored. I don't remember ever being bored.

Nelle Frakes, 71, Perry County

We had jobs to do. I remember learning to work at a very early age and I never begrudged that. In fact, I never gave it a second thought; I just thought that everybody had to work. To this day I appreciate more than anything that they taught me how to work. Good honest work never hurt anybody.

Judi Merkel, 34, Adams County

PLAY AT
HOME

I lived in my own little world for about the first four years of my life. I had imaginary characters, and my best friend was Shoby Shay.

Shoby Shay lived under a bush out by the side of the house, and we did everything together. She listened to all of my problems. If I was corrected, she heard all about my problems. I listened very intently, and somehow or another, that little Shoby always talked back. We played house and we did many, many things together. That was my first friend.

A little girl moved in down the street when I was three. She was my best friend. We did everything together.

We would play hopscotch; we played with marbles; [we swung] in the old rope swing; we loved to climb trees; and we skated. I can still see her skating. Straight skating was a bore, so she would put her arms inside her dress and skate like a sack.

And we played tag; we played house; we played with paper dolls; we played ball; and made doll clothes.

We walked miles and miles and miles, just going from one end of town to the other. We had no fear of anybody disturbing us. We would take each street; and the railroad tracks was another place we loved to play.

But my parents provided the home base. They provided toys and places to play and things to do.

Jean Brechbill, 65, DeKalb County

We lived in a small town. That was before we had automobiles and we played on the street corner in the summertime. The boys and the girls, we'd get out there and we played Black Man and Hide and Go Seek in the evenings. After supper in the wintertime, why we'd get together, the neighbor children. There was one boy I remember that he could sing, and he'd come and we'd sing. We'd have popcorn and apples and play checkers and dominoes and Old Maid.

Jane White, 78, Owen County

We went roller skating. Oh, we went roller skating. We'd go up town and we'd roller skate around the courthouse. That was the big thing when I was growing up, was to roller skate around the courthouse. There was nothing to interfere with you and you could really skate, and pert near every day we'd go up there. I don't know how many skates I wore out, to tell you the truth.

LaVerda Shearer, 56, Whitley County

We lived in an interesting neighborhood where there was a lot of children. There were 44 children in our block. They would get together in all sorts of projects. They liked to play out in the street. Traffic wasn't anything in those days. They'd play right out in the street under the street lights and have great crowds of them together. We enjoyed it very much.

Camille Hey, 89, Shelby County

A family of dolls and their owner.
Submitted by an Extension Homemaker

We lived three doors from the school. We had a mob of kids there all the time. My mother and father were most cordial with our friends. They loved having children there and the yard was always full.

Behind our house was a vacant lot with a mulberry tree and we played there—mobs of children from all over town, all the time. The whole summer we filled the lot. I remember it as a huge lot, but now as we look at it, it was one one-house lot.

The mulberry tree was good for staining your clothes, but I spent many hours reading up in the mulberry tree. We all enjoyed it.

Mary Helms, 45, Franklin County

Pulaski was a very small town, and there were two croquet sets in town. My folks happened to have one, so we always had plenty of company. They wouldn't come and play unless I played with them, so I grew up playing croquet a lot.

In the evenings they would just come in and sing songs around the piano and have a good time. My mother would probably serve popcorn which we raised ourself. It didn't cost anything.

Virgie Bowers, 81, Pulaski County

In our big old barn that was on the back of our lot, we would dress up in play clothes and we had real curtains at the window of the barn. We had doll furniture that my dad had made out of boxes for us. So in this barn we had a whole city that we could play with. We had a house. We had the bedroom and we had the living room and we had the kitchen. We had the church, we had a grocery store, and sometimes we had a post office. This barn provided an awful lot of my play.

Jean Brechbill, 65, DeKalb County

I didn't have no one but myself. My mother's children all died before me—she had five. I was the only one left, so I was lonely. If I hadn't had neighbor children to come and play with I wouldn't have knowed what to do with myself, I guess.

We always had plays. We would get up plays of all kinds, just little skits and things like that. We would have them up in our barn. We had a great big loft up there and it was a real nice floor. We even waxed the floor and put a Victrola up there and danced afterwards.

Ozetta Sullivan, 72, Harrison County

We'd run across the fields to visit our girl and boy friends when Mother would say, "Well, you have no work to do today; you can go visiting." Many, many times we laid down on our bellies and drank out of tile ditches. The water was clean then. It really was—it was clear as crystal. Today it's so polluted.

Beulah Grinstead, 68, Hamilton County

After you were old enough to go to school, you would have girl friends come home with you and stay all night, but not when you were younger, you didn't.

Opal Whitsett, 84, Scott County

I had lots of girl friends and it was fun to stay at their house all night because most of them lived in town and I lived in the country. And when they came home with me, we rode horseback, skated and waded in Hanna's creek and just had fun as country kids.

Gleda Stevens, Union County

What did you do for fun?
In the summer we had playhouses outside on the ground. We had certain things left from year to year that we put up with kind of little fences around them, and we would have our playhouses in there.

We made mud pies. When rhubarb came along, or fresh beets, we would cut the stems off beets and make rhubarb pies, mud pies, and they were beautiful (laughs).

I still have the first doll that I had. It was store-bought, with a china head. I named it Emma, after Emma Downen. I thought she was the most beautiful woman that I had ever seen, so my doll was Emma. We played with dolls in the house.

Audrey Blackburn, 86, Posey County

Opal: We played out under the old maple tree. We didn't have the toys to play with like they do now.

Juanita: Our play houses had broken dishes.

Opal: Yes, broken dishes and you would make your tables and things out of bricks and shingles and anything you could put your broken dishes on.

Opal Whitsett, 81, and Juanita Hunter, 84, Scott County

How lonely and dull my life as a child would seem to children now. We lived on a back road, not even gravelled. There were three families on the road, but none of them had small children for me to play with. The nearest children were a mile away, going across the fields and much farther by road. Remember, our only transportation was by horse and buggy. My father did not have a car until 1917, after I had graduated from high school.

So, when I played, I played alone and there had to be a lot of make-believe. My favorite pastime was playing house with my dolls out under a big old crab apple tree. I still have a beautiful German-made

doll that I received for Christmas when I was ten years old. I think I
played with that doll through most of my high school years.

Ruth Snyder, 83, Marshall County

I remember one time that Susie [friend] had an old hen stole her nest
out and hatched out some little chickens and she [Susie] told me I
could have those little chicks, if I wanted them. There was about seven
or eight of them.

So I did. I took them home and put them in a box and kept them in
the yard and fed them. At night, when it came time for them to settle

Pets were an important part of growing up
in the rural and small-town setting.
Submitted by Kosciusko County

down for the night, I would go out and sit down on the step, and they
would all come and get in my lap, and cuddle down, like chickens will
when they want to go to roost. Then I'd put them in their box and
cover them up.

I think they all lived, and when they got almost full grown, I would
go out in the yard, and they'd fly up on my shoulder. They were real
pets. I was just like the old mother hen to them.

We had a nice dog. Old Tip. He was Roy's [brother] dog; he trained
him. He would do most anything. When Roy was in service [WWI], he

would get a furlough and he would come as far as Springfield [on the train] and then walk out home. And Tip, before he could even see him, he knew it. He would go way down the road to meet him. He would get his scent, or something, and he knew he was coming.

And Roy used to, when it come time to get the milk cows in, he'd say, "Tip, go get the cows," and away he'd go, off to the pasture, and bring them in, without anybody with him.

And I remember kittens. I'd always hunt around for them when they were born and I would find them, usually in the haymow. And then I would stay with them so much they would get tame. Then when they'd come up to the house, I would dress them up in my doll clothes and put them in a doll buggy and in bed. Put dresses on, and bonnets. They didn't mind. They were so tame they didn't care (laughs). They'd lay there and sleep.

Anna Martin, 80, White County

We had a bulldog called Madge. Mother would put a note on her, and tell her to go find Arch. [She would leave] and back she would come with a note from Arch. She had found him.

Phyllis Frank, 79, DeKalb County

We sold buttermilk at 10¢ a gallon and we bought Horatio Alger books—that would have been in 1912 or 1914, something like that.

I thought that was boy's books.

I guess it was, but we loved them. And Elsie Dinsmore books. When they put a little library in our country school we went to at that time, we asked the teacher if she was going to get some Elsie Dinsmore books. She said, "*NO*, we're getting books here to save you from that kind of literature." (laughs)

Horatio Alger always had a moral to it. It was a good boy who was very poor, and a bad boy who was very rich. And at the end of the book they exchanged places. Right after that came *Freckles* and *Girl of the Limberlost,* so Gene Stratton Porter was our next love.

And Mother used to read to us while we peeled apples or done something of that kind.

But I always loved to read. I would go hide and read.

Well, it must have been encouraged. Your parents didn't discourage you?

No, no. My father was a Bible student. He didn't even finish grade school, but he loved to read and study. Oh, yes, we were encouraged to read—if we got our chores done first. (chuckles)

Neva Schlatter, 79, Pulaski County

When I went to school, I was quite a student. I like books and I loved to read. When my mother expected me to be doing work, I would be behind the door in the bedroom with a book. My sister would find me and she'd tell on me.

Mary Summers, 69, Newton County

I loved to read. Most generally, when I was a kid, I read about a book a day.

Anna Surfus, 85, DeKalb County

My Aunt Linnie Monroe had been a teacher. She was one to share. She saw to it that we had the Youth Companion in those days. That was the only children's magazine that we knew about. They paid a dollar a year and my father had to pay the other 75¢ to get it. And when it came, all four of us, we put it on the floor and all four of us tried to read it at the same time.

Mabel Bobbitt, 88, Shelby County

I had a happy childhood. I was the youngest of four children, and they never paid too much attention to me. They let me go wild in my own sweet way. I can remember I was just in my element—I would go get in the swing with a book and a kitty.

Margaret Gibson, 88, Cass County

I didn't have too many books at home, but I read a lot of books out of the school libraries. And this teacher we had, he had a lot of books himself. And he would loan those books to the older kids. So we had quite a few of his books around there. I don't remember the names, but some of them Dad didn't think they were fit for me to read (laughs). He would say, "Now, girls, you can't read that book." And he would give them back to the man they belonged to. He was worse than Mother about things like that. I don't know what he would think of the books nowadays.

Anna Martin, 80, White County

We were not allowed to read "reading circle" books, as my father thought they would interfere with our lessons. I will have to admit I kept books hid in the hayloft and when I had time I would go up there and read. I remember *Lena Rivers* (how I suffered with her), also *Bears of Blue River* and *The Call of the Wild.* I loved books, and with them I escaped into another lovely world.

Violet David, 82, Brown County

I remember the first radio I ever heard. It was a crystal set, and you had to have earphones. There was only one person that had a radio in Laotto and everybody would go over there. They would take their turns listening to that radio with the earphones.

That must have been fun.

It was, but you'd only get to listen a little while because there were so many that wanted to listen (laughs).

Hazel Norden, 76, DeKalb County

The old battery radio was a real joy of mine. We had one of the first. Jack Armstrong and Orphan Annie and The Shadow Knows took over our imaginations. I can remember calling Daddy at work some evenings and telling him that we just had to have a new battery, and quickly, because the programs would soon be on, and I didn't know what was happening, because it would just fade away. And so we kept up with what was happening in the lives of Amos and Andy, and Lum and Abner, and Gracie and George.

Jean Brechbill, 65, DeKalb County

Did you have any heroes or heroines?

When I stop to think about it—I guess Jo in *Little Women*. I was a big fan of Jack Armstrong, The All American Boy, too, and those other radio people. I never missed Little Orphan Annie. I drank my Ovaltine like a good girl and then sent away for those Secret Decoder pins. What memories!!

Mary Ann Moore, 57, Hendricks County

My idol was my big brother. He had a motorcycle and he would take me a ride, and I can remember my mom standing out in the yard, screaming "Bring her back!"

Opal Gallagher, 72, Shelby County

We had this huge barn about fifty feet long and we had a swing that went way up in the rafters of this barn. The hay rope was knotted around that and that swing would swing clear from one end of the mow to the other.

We'd have a ball down there. We would swing, and sometimes we'd get a ladder across between the two hay mows, and we'd act like we were acrobats. My brother got hung up there one time by his feet. He said, "I can hang by my feet like other people can." He was hanging by one rung of that ladder by his feet, and he couldn't get himself back up. My other brother and I were too short to reach him, and we didn't know what we were going to do. He said, "Beulah, pile straw under me just as fast as you can. And Darrel, you run to the house quick and see if you can get Mom down here." Well, Mom came just in time. He was just about ready to slip and fall.

Beulah Grinstead, 68, Hamilton County

Growing up as a child I was a tremendous tomboy. I had a favorite place to get away from it all. We had a branch [creek] that went through our farm and they cut a big old sycamore tree down and left a wonderful stump to sit on and contemplate.

I was lucky enough growing up to have a girl that lived next door that was only a year older than I and we were together constantly. What we didn't do, no one could even think of. Our folks used to worry whenever a storm would come up, because if we could find out there was one coming, we would run off way down in the pasture, where we couldn't hear them holler, and climb the highest trees, as high as we could go, so the wind would blow us in the swaying trees.

Doris Chapman, 46, Daviess County

In the summertime, if a big storm came up, our pond would be all full of water. It'd be maybe two or three feet deep. The neighbors would all come over with their old clothes on, and us kids would get out there and we'd pretend we were swimming. We really had a good time with that. But in the wintertime it was more fun than that, because it would freeze over and then we would take our kitchen chairs out. The girls would sit on the chairs, and the boys had their skates on, and they would skate and push us from one side of the pond to the other. Mother couldn't understand why her chair legs got so short. We really had them worn off.

Masa Scheerer, 82, Huntington County

We lived in a small house on the banks of the Tippecanoe River; and that river was a part of our life. One thing, it furnished the fish for a lot of our meat meals, because at that time it was clear and there were a lot of fish in the river. You could go down and fish for about twenty minutes to a half hour and have plenty of fish for a big fish dinner. We thoroughly enjoyed our fishing, and we enjoyed boating a lot. That was one of our pleasures in the summertime.

Did you learn to swim?

Yes, I learned to swim. Almost everyone did who lived along the river. That was one of the summer pastimes, boating and swimming. And in the wintertime we did ice skating.

Virgie Bowers, 81, Pulaski County

When I was growing up, we swam in the river and the creeks. I was always afraid in the river, and I wouldn't go out very far. There were stepoffs in it. When I would go in the creek, I would take a stick and use it in front of me to see where the stepoffs were.

Also, the bathing suits were altogether different. The first bathing suit I had was like bloomers, then a skirt, a waist, a cap and even rubber sandals.Think how skimpy they are now!

Evelyn Buchanan, 78, Scott County

When we were growing up, we played along the Ohio River. I think now if we lived some place like that and the children wanted to play someplace like that, I would say, "No, no, no!"

What seemed all right when we are a child doesn't seem all right when we are an adult.

We played along the river. We would wave at those big boats. We thought they came from nowhere and were going into the next world.

Juanita Harden, 49, Bartholomew County

One of my most enjoyable summers I wasn't old enough to work, but old enough to take care of my younger brothers and sisters. We would go to the woods and explore. Many times Mother would help us pack a picnic lunch and we would stay all day.

Across the fence was a waterfall. It was very intriguing, the place we wanted to play. Someone was always slipping in the stream. It was sort of nice getting all wet in the summer.

There was a bluff where the rocks had fossils in them, and Indian beads. It was hard to find beads with holes all the way through so we could make necklaces. All the fox holes had to be investigated.

In the spring there were crows feet, windflowers, hepatica, blood root (it "bleeds" when you pick it), sweet Williams, bluebells, shooting stars, jack-in-the-pulpit (if anyone ever talks you into tasting the bulb, you will never forget it), and many more flowers. We would pick a bouquet for Mother. I was so happy when I found sweet William blooming, as they were Mother's favorite. Mother would thank us, making us feel we had done something wonderful for her. She put the flowers in a vase and set them where everyone could see them. Never was anything said about the flowers being wilted by the time we got back home with them.

Poppie's woods had the best grapevines, very strong and well anchored in the tall trees. Of course, the ones that swung out over the bluff were the most fun.

In the fall, there were persimmons to gather, also hickory nuts and walnuts. First you must crack and eat some nuts from all of the trees so you would know which ones are the best.

As Christmas season approached, we gathered bittersweet and cedar with blue berries. Tom got the mistletoe that grew high up in the trees. These made beautiful decorations and made the entire house smell of cedar.

Helen Ridge, Crawford County

Did you live a good deal of your child life outside?
Yes, all outside. That's what I think about people in the city and how in the world they do, all cooped up. No, I spent my time mostly outside.

Alvah Watson, 97, Allen County

Did you go to the woods in the spring to pick flowers?
Oh, yes, that was our main jaunt, going down to the woods. We were there when the flowers would come up in the spring and in the fall when we'd walk through the leaves. We used to pick wild strawberries and there used to be some trees laying down, and we used to walk the trees. That used to be our fun and excitement.

Hazel Norden, 76, DeKalb County

Part of our farm was woods, and in the spring we went down there every Sunday and picked flowers. We always had flowers from the time the first little spring beauties came up. We had dozens of varieties of wildflowers, a lot of them were scarce.

Mabel Hunter, 70, Jasper County

In the spring we went barefoot, which was a great joy. We went out to gather dogwood, redbud and many kinds of wild flowers in the spring, and made bouquets for our mother.
We built leaf houses in the woods for shelter and play houses.

Garnet Parsley, 63, Brown County

Everybody wanted to get rid of his woods. But the woods was wonderful. We'd spend our time in the woods. We'd make our swings out there. We'd skin-a-cat and climb a tree and all those things. The woods was wonderful.
But now it's gone and we took all the timber away. I think of all those great big long trees rolled up and on fire. At night you could see a fire here and one over there, all over the county, where people were clearing their land.
We tried, my father tried, to have three acres every year added to the farm land. And my brothers used to get so tired of picking roots and things. Getting the ground ready for grain.

Alvah Watson, 97, Allen County

All that is changed now. It was nothing but farm land all through here, but it's all built up. It's not in the country now, not like it was then.

Ellen Doss, 34, Clark County

Tell us about that tree in the front yard, that catalpa tree.
Well, I can't remember when it wasn't there. It's just about dead. There are two big arms that goes and makes a V. I always called it my victory tree.
Then you played under the tree, and so did your children?
My brothers and sisters, and children and grandchildren. I've got pictures of the grandchildren sitting up in that V.
Did you climb up in it?
Oh, lots of times. I was a tomboy. It still has leaves and foliage on it every year and I won't let them cut it down, because I played under it all my life. I expect there is people that goes by and wonders why Agnes doesn't cut that tree down, but I'm not a-going to.

It'll probably be there as long as I live. I'll not do away with it. Like the old house where we live now, we just hope it will stand until we're gone. It's part of me.

Agnes Bell, 85, Hamilton County

HOLIDAYS

What about Easter?
Mother would always dye eggs when us children weren't around and each one would go out the night before and pick grass. Mother had a lot of bread pans, and she would give us the baking pans and we would take them out, fill them with grass, and then we would line them up along the wall.

When we woke up Easter morning, there would be our eggs in the basket. We never got a whole lot of candy or anything like that. Our baskets had eggs in them.

Come to find out when we got older, we didn't have dye like they do now to dye eggs. You used onion peelings to make a brown and you used grass to make them green. I forget what kind of flower or weed it was that you used to make it purple.

Edna Klinstiver, 58, Floyd County

One of the things at our house was on the first day of April. There was always salt in the sugar bowl, and there was a lot of faces made when oatmeal was eaten.

Juanita Hunter, 81, Scott County

About the biggest holdiay for me was what we called Decoration Day. We always went to the town of Greenwood and they would have a big parade and the bands, and they would have a speaker, of course. It was after Easter, and we would get to dress up in our Easter clothes. It was a big day for us.

Opal Gallagher, 72, Shelby County

Fourth of July was another holiday we eagerly awaited. We usually had a picnic with games, contests, picnic lunch and ice cream, soda pop, candy, cracker jack and all those treats we only got on very rare occasions.

Mabel Hunter, 70, Jasper County

The Fourth of July was a time for homemade ice cream and fireworks. That was a time when the whole neighborhood went together. The young people a lot of times would go out to Lake Cicott on a hayride and they would have a picnic and swimming.

Margaret Gibson, 87, Cass County

On the Fourth of July they had ball games all over town. Every park would have a ball game going on.

You could buy firecrackers then and everyone was shooting off firecrackers. Then you could watch fireworks. The country club used to always have fireworks, and then at Foster Park downtown, they had huge fireworks displays.

Betty Alvey, 60, Howard County

On the Fourth of July we would have our own fireworks at night. Every neighbor had them and we watched everyone else's, as we sort of went in a circle around the neighborhood. That way we didn't all see them at the same time. We had our fireworks in the front yard, on the road.

Florence Carson, 58, LaPorte County

On Halloween we played pranks on the neighbors and stretched rope across the sidewalks. People wore hats then, and it would just catch their hats and throw them back. We would be hiding and watching. I don't remember that we ever got caught.

Evelyn Buchanan, 78, Scott County

When I was a kid, there was a sawmill over at Brownsville, and they had three or four log wagons up there. Every Halloween, some of the kids would bring those wagons down and pile them up, one on top of the other, in front of the school door. They had to work hard to do it.

Of course, they moved every toilet and every gate in town, but that was the main thing—to get those log wagons down there.

Maud Sloneker, 90, Fayette County

We had a community of friends around, and we would have lots of fun. Like at Halloween, we'd all get together and dress up. I remember one time we went to my folks and my dad was going to scare us by shooting up in the air, and he shot up and he hurt his shoulder (laughs).

My dad was lots of fun. One time he dressed up to resemble a fat lady, putting bosoms on and everything, and he had a [false] face on. Dad chewed tobacco and he forgot he had his tobacco in his mouth, and he had his mask on, and that gave him away (laughs).

Phyllis Frank, 79, DeKalb County

We would dress up for Halloween and go to the neighbors' houses. We'd never trick or treat. We'd never heard of trick or treat. We'd just go and have them guess you. We'd make our mother dress up and she'd go along because she got such a kick out of it. We'd tell her, "Now, don't giggle." She'd get in there and get giggling and everybody knew right away who she was (chuckles). I did that even after I was married. One time my uncle said, "The only ones that come anymore is you, so we know it is you guys." (chuckle) It was just for the fun of dressing up and going.

Dorothy Hoffman, 59, Adams County

At Christmas we didn't have stockings to hang, because we had our one pair on, but we would leave our plates on the table, and we would put our names on them. And the next morning we'd hurry around to scc what we had. I remember one time we had half a fig. And maybe mother would have some of those little old-fashioned sugar candies and she would cut them in two, so she'd have enough to go around.

And always our Christmas presents were things that Mother would make. She always had wrist bands to wear to school, she'd say to keep your pulse warm. And she'd make us stockings. Maybe you'd get a pair of pants you had a year ago, that she'd remodeled. And we always spent Christmas Eve and Christmas morning at home.

Everybody went to Grandfather's and we'd have a big dinner. He'd have a bedroom shut off and he had a young cedar in there, and the doors closed. About 10 o'clock in the morning when all the children had arrived, he'd give each grandchild a firecracker and they would go out by a tree and they'd shoot these firecrackers off, and then they'd go in the house.

And at noon he would get my mother and all her sisters and the older folks would set at the table, and the young ones would have to stand back. We would stand around, as hungry as could be, and we would wonder if there'd by any left, and what we'd get.

Then when they got through with their dinner and their talking around the table, why they would leave and we would sit down. And Grandmother, the first thing she'd do she'd put parsnips on your plate and say, "I tell you, they are good for your health." But we didn't want parsnips. We wanted turkey. But we had to take what they gave us.

Then in the afternoon, they'd open up the room with the tree and my mother and her sisters would exchange some little things they had made and that was their Christmas.

Alvah Watson, 97, Allen County

We always had Christmas at Grandma Bonnell's. We'd have a Santa Claus and had a big Christmas tree—in the parlor, mind you. That was the one time we'd get in the parlor. My aunt played the organ, and we sang Christmas carols. I don't think she was very good on the organ, because sometimes she only played with one hand, and sometimes she played with both hands. But the organ was always sort of a mystery to us, because we didn't get in there except at Christmas time.

Grandpa always had a stalk of bananas, a crate of oranges, and we would take apples. My mother always made popcorn balls; put them in a 50 pound lard tin and took them.

We never exchanged gifts. We just got together and had a fun time. And I look back and I think that was probably some of the happiest times we ever had.

Mildred Weaver, 64, Pulaski County

We always went to five o'clock mass at St. Mary's on Christmas morning. But before we went, Mother would have the Christmas tree lighted and ready, and then she would blow a little horn. That horn had the sweetest tone to it that I think I ever heard. Then we'd come down, my youngest sister first, then me, then the rest, in stairsteps. We went in and looked at the tree. We saw we had presents and there wasn't a whole lot of time then, but we were satisfied, then we could go to church. We would come home and then we opened our presents.

But when my mother would come to the foot of the steps and blow that horn, we thought that was something. That was Christmas.

Mary Flispart, 81, Floyd County

When I was a child, the Christmas celebration was, really, just in your home, and the church. And if there was business of any kind to take care of, they went right ahead and took care of it.

Eldo Bell, 86, Spencer County

Our family didn't stress holidays too much. My father, while he loved his family and would have done anything for them, he didn't believe in all these little extras that people participate in nowadays. He was sort of a Puritan type, I would say.

Ruth Snyder, 83, Marshall County

My dad's family, Grandpa brought home a whole stalk of bananas and they was their treat for the holidays. That was their Christmas.

Sharon Windhorst, 35, Fayette County

Did you have a Christmas tree?

No, I had the first Christmas tree in the family when I got married. No, my mother never had a Christmas tree. Christmas at home, each kid had a chair lined up and we hung our stockings on a chair back. And Santa Claus came and left things. And when we got older, we still played, because you had to keep the little ones inspired.

Edna Winter, 74, Pulaski County

We used to make a lot of our Christmas decorations. We would color the paper, cut it into little strips and make chains and would string them from one corner of the room to the other corner for decorations. We did not always have a Christmas tree.

Where were your presents left?

We would set out a chair with our name on it. Santa Claus would leave our gifts on our particular chair. I remember when Santa Claus would come, my father always had to be some place else. One time he had an old sick horse out in the barn, and while he was gone, Santa Claus came in. I was never the least bit suspicious.

Ruth Bateman, 63, Daviess County

In the fall we gathered bittersweet which grows wild in the hills and saved it to decorate the Christmas tree.

Garnet Parsley, 63, Brown County

I remember that I used to fix strings of cranberries and popcorn to put on the Christmas tree and we had candles on the little holders that you just clamped onto the tree. If you lit them, you had to stay right there, because of the danger of the tree catching on fire. I remember a couple of times when it did, but they put it out right away.

Evelyn Buchanan, 78, Scott County

We had a big Christmas tree, not an artificial one and it usually reached to the ceiling. Mother and Daddy would put it up after us children went to bed and they had candles on it which were in little holders that clamped on the tree. They had old-fashioned ornaments— a lot of them was homemade. Then you made rings of [paper] chain strung around it and then strung popcorn and put it around the tree.

Then, on Christmas morning, when we all got up, they would light the candles on the tree for five or ten minutes and then throughout the day, it would get lit a couple of times and on Christmas night.

Edna Klinstiver, 57, Floyd County

In those days there were candles on the trees, but they were just lit for maybe ½ hour, then they would blow them out because they were afraid those old pine trees would catch on fire. There had been different houses that had burnt down just on account of the Christmas trees.

Neva Schlatter, 79, Pulaski County

When I was a child, we had a Christmas tree decorated with popcorn and berries. We had lighted candles that we put on for just a little while. They were candles burning, not electric, for we didn't have electricity then.

We didn't get very many gifts. If we got candy, an orange, an apple, and maybe a story book or a doll in our stocking, we thought we were just rich. That was the extent. There was very little spent on Christmas. We really couldn't afford it and no one else did, so you didn't expect it.

Emma Baker, 78, Scott County

I always got a doll on Christmas. And Mom and Dad would say that they wanted to visit the neighbors on Christmas Eve. (We always had our Christmas on Christmas Eve.) And that was an excuse so Santa could come while we were gone. When we got back, my Christmas would all be in a rocking chair. We didn't have a tree. We just put everything in a rocking chair.

A Christmas tree hung with popcorn
garlands and a few ornaments fascinates
this youngster.
Submitted by Newton County

Were your gifts wrapped?
   Yes, she always wrapped them, but I don't remember what kind of paper she used. We didn't have pretty paper then.

Was your home decorated at Christmas time?
Well, yes, with what we had. You cut cedar off the tree and we
would have popcorn, you know.
Cleo Borders, 75, Martin County

We always had company at Christmastime. And Christmas morning
we expected a gift. We'd write letters to "Santy Claus," although we
really knew there was no Santa Claus. We would joke, more or less,
about it. We would get, perhaps, a bracelet, a ring, or something of
that sort in our stockings. And usually we had an orange and some
candy. We never expected a lot of packages. I don't know of anybody
in that day that did.
Neva Schlatter, 79, Pulaski County

I remember one Christmas Ray [brother] made me a little washtub
and wringer, and some little clothes pins. He made the little washtub
out of a wooden keg that he had sawed in half. He made the little
wringer; he had the rollers and a little crank on it and you could turn
it. And he had whittled the little clothespins out of a piece of wood.
Anna Martin, 80, White County

My brother and I dug ginseng and yellow root and sold it to the
druggist to get money to buy Christmas presents for our father and
mother. We would walk to Georgetown and go to a notion store. We
would have such a hard time deciding. We usually ended up with a
dish for our mother and a pocket knife for father.
Violet David, 79, Brown County

We'd have oranges in the toe of our stocking and peanuts and
candy. And then, sticking out of the top of the stocking, would be a
doll. And we always had dolls with china heads, with black painted
hair, and we thought they were wonderful. But one year Mother got us
dolls that went to sleep and had what we said was natural hair. And
these dolls were probably about eight inches long. They were very
small. But they were the most wonderful dolls you ever saw! And to
think that they'd go to sleep!
Erma Agnew, 88, Decatur County

Usually one or two presents is all that you got. I can remember we
got Bibles one time. The Christmas before the flood of 1937 we had
gotten a doll for each one of us girls. Daddy tried to save them; took a
boat out to get them, but you couldn't get in far enough to get the
dolls. They was afraid to go inside the house, afraid it might take off

[with him inside]. I remember the Christmas after the flood, Daddy walked to New Albany and brought home five pounds of chocolate drops and five pounds of oranges, and that was it.

Edna Klinstiver, 58, Floyd County

How old were you when you believed in Santa Claus?

Oh, I believed in that old boy until I was five years old. Now my sister could find anything, and she said to me, "Do you know that we're going to each get a beautiful big doll for Christmas? And it's dressed up so pretty."

We would always have a plate on the table and in the morning it would be all full of candy and oranges and bananas, and then our toys would be right beside of it. So this year, in 1905, we girls got the most beautiful dolls I ever saw. They were this bisque head and curly hair, and my mother had them dressed so pretty that she had made. We took good care of them.

Neva Schlatter, 79, Pulaski County

One time at Christmas time we had been out to the barn, doing the milking, and we had taken the milk in the house to put in them gallon crocks, and we were doing it and Santa Claus looked in the window!

We all had to kneel down and say an Our Father and a Hail Mary. But then a few days later we was out in the barn and we had a big wooden box there, where we had oats. We looked in there, and here was Santa Claus' suit, which kind of gave things away. We were just about at that age where we didn't know for sure, but we knew after that.

Martha Werner, 63, Franklin County

When I was a little chubby girl of about five or six at home, I had a big story to tell. We always had a little Christmas tree on the sewing machine, decorated with popcorn strings or some candy. And we always got something, one thing, that we really wanted. We always had a big dinner on Christmas Day.

I got in my head when I was five or six that there wasn't no real Santa Claus, and I told my parents that. My father was sitting in an easy chair and he laughed, but my mother said, "If you don't think there is a Santa Claus, it will be too bad; because Santa Claus is love."

I didn't understand that, but I hadn't any more than said that, that same Christmas, when Santa Claus knocked on the door. My daddy opened the door, and there stood Santa Claus. I raced for the bedroom and crawled under the bed. I thought I had done something real smart in saying there wasn't any Santa Claus, and here he was.

The bed was slatted and low, extremely low, and I got fast. Santa Claus stayed a little bit and then he left. My father had to come in and take me by the legs and pull real hard to get me out.

You believed in Santa Claus after that, didn't you?

Yes, I did for a few more years. But I don't know, I believe there is a Santa Claus yet; because, like my mother said, he is love.

Clara Nichols, 79, Wabash County

GROWING UP
AT MY SCHOOL

"I went to a one-room school, with all grades.
We had a big stove in the school that you fired with wood.
Everybody wanted to carry the water
from Mr. Livingston's pump.
We would take the bucket and bring the water back.
We had one cup and everybody drank out of that one cup."
Blanche Heaton, 82, Greene County

All the pupils of District School No. 9
pose together in front of their one-room
schoolhouse. Their young teacher stands
among them, while the township trustee
stands slightly apart. It is February 11,
according to the hand-lettered sign.
Submitted by Newton County

THE
SCHOOLHOUSE

Did Huntington have several one-room schools then?

Oh, yes, just about every two miles. Where we lived we could go to five different schools. We had our choice.

What was school like then?

We had all eight grades in a school and one teacher to teach us. We'd start in what we called the Primer class, and the next was first and second. And they'd teach all eight grades through one day.

Most generally in the morning we'd have reading. We always started with reading and then arithmetic and on down. And we'd have recess about 10:00 in the morning, then maybe we'd have our physiology and English.

Did you eat at school?

Yes, we always had to carry a lunch. All had lunch pails. We'd go in that room and at the back they'd have shelves and we all set our lunch pails up there.

And we had this one stove in the middle of the room. And the ones close to the stove got too hot and the ones (laughing) on the outside would be freezing. We wore big heavy clothes and boots—shoes that laced clean up to our knees.

That was quite a responsibility to be going two miles to school, and bundling up in frigid weather. How old was the oldest pupil?

I think he was about 17 or 18.

Was there several families involved then in the school?

Oh, yes. We had 40 or 50 children. They was a lot of us.

And one teacher taught that number of students.

All around the school for two miles, they come in.

Was there another school that you went up to the twelfth grade?

Well, you had to take an examination to get into high school and I never took that, because I quit school. My mother was kind of poorly and I had to help do the work.

I said I know I can write and figure and read a little bit. Now children get out of school and can't even do that.

Cora Keplinger, 80, Huntington County

I was younger than I should have been to go to school. I would have been five in January, so I really started school when I was four.

They didn't have a law about it. I had a best buddy who was starting and I wanted to start, too. I did know my letters and my numbers, so my mother did allow me to go.

How old were you when you started high school, then?

I was 11. I had even skipped a grade and that is something. I wouldn't recommend it, as I really wasn't that mature physically, but I kept up with my grades. I finished fourth in the county.

Birdena Day, 61, Wells County

When I was five years old I started to school. I skipped the first grade. As my mother said, I always went around with a book and pencil in my hand. So when I was five years old, I was in the second grade.

I graduated from common school (as it was called in those days). It was a one-room school called Smyrna School. There were 20 pupils and they had all eight grades.

I remember the first day of school the neighbor's girl took me to school. I had always been afraid of the boogey man, and when she came after me, I thought she was the boogey man, so I ran home as fast as I could. But after that it was O.K. and I liked school.

Ethel Meyer, 78, Ripley County

My first day of school I was seven and half years old, because when I lived up the country I would have had to walk two miles. It was too far for me to walk. So I didn't go to school until we moved to Rockville.

I moved there in the middle of winter and started in the first grade. Then another girl and I took two or three days a week training in the summer, and we moved on into the second grade.

Hazel Thomas, 81, Parke County

I went to No. 11 school in Jackson Township. It was one room and had all eight grades in one room.

Do you remember your first day of school?

Oh, yes, I remember it very much. It was quite a thrill. We went with our older sister, my sister and I. Our teacher's first name was Mary, and we called her Miss Mary. We just thought she was an angel from heaven.

Theresa Bramblett, 75, Parke County

I went to school in a one-room schoolhouse. They had double seats in that schoolhouse and a boy sat with me in the double seat and he was very mischievous.

Later they built the school building there and we had two rooms up and two rooms down, so that is where I got my grade school.

I graduated from Kokomo High School on June 10, 1910, and I was married on June 15, 1910. Our daughter was born in 1912. When she went to school she had the same schoolteacher that I had when I went to school at Hemlock School years before.

Edna Vandenbark, 92, Howard County

At the Barger School, half of the room was seats; the other half was where the stove was and where we played. There were eight grades, but we had maybe one or two or three per grade. That was all the kids there was in that school.

Dorothy Hoffman, 54, Adams County

And there were eight grades in that one little school?

Yes, maybe there wouldn't be any pupils in one grade, but then maybe there would only be one [in a grade], but we all went.

Thelma Fox, 74, Shelby County

What was your school room like?

It was just one big room with two doors facing west, which was the front of the schoolhouse. It had a big heating stove in the center and all the seats were double. That is, two pupils sat in each seat. And the desk was divided so where we kept our books underneath, each one had his own place. But all the seats were double.

And at the back of the room, in the center, was a big sort of a cabinet. It was a big cupboard, really, and that was the library, for all the books we had. Most of the time they were Alger books, Horatio Alger books.

And then on each side of this cabinet were the hooks where we hung our coats. One side was for the boys and one side for the girls.

You didn't have coatrooms?

Oh, no. Just hooks. We just put our coats [on hooks] and set our dinnerbuckets on the floor under our coat.

Anna Martin, 80, White County

Was this all grades in one room at Catlin?

We had two rooms, but it had those big doors that rolled up and they could put it all as one room when we had our plays and things.

Was that heated with one stove?

No, we had a stove in each room where it was divided. There was the first four grades on one side and four grades on the other side.

Laura Drake, 72, Parke County

My family moved near town for my fourth year in school and I missed the older students. It was at first very strange to be in a room with children all of the same age and size.

Bea Shuel, 74, Gibson County

We moved back to Clay Township and I attended school there. Gee, what a big school. One room was bigger than the whole schoolhouse at Dongola. There were four big rooms downstairs and a hallway going in all directions. I was lost for three or four weeks.

I didn't know for two or three years what was up the big stairway on the second floor. I would see a host of big boys and girls go up and down the stairs.

Marjorie Malott, 67, Pike County

At noon there was two kids that had to take turns going down to Mr. and Mrs. John Hegel's to get a bucket of water. This was our drinking water. When we came back, we had to be careful that we didn't spill it. There were about 20 kids in school and we had one tin cup that sat on the shelf beside the water bucket and we all drank out of one tin cup. Seems like it didn't hurt us, we were tough.

Alma Knecht, 78, Wabash County

Where did you get your water?
We had a well out in the schoolyard. We had individual cups, folding cups. We were real modern to have those.

Icil Hughes, 78, Grant County

[My] school had about 40 children in one room, with a pot-bellied stove. We did have a coat room and in the coat room was your water bucket and dipper. Everybody had to have a tin cup and had to have a place to put your tin cup, so you really didn't drink after anybody and nobody drunk after you. But you did have a common wash pan. If you'd been to the outside "plumbing" you came inside and had to wash your hands in the common ordinary wash pan.

Mary Ann Hoskins, Grant County

And if we had to go to the rest room, we had to go out in the cold weather. You had to go outside. We always had to hold up two fingers if we had to go out. Oooh! The well was out east of the schoolhouse and they had a building out east of the school where they kept their wood and coal. And the teacher was the janitor.

Helen Shockey, 80, Grant County

Then the teacher lived quite a distance from the schoolhouse. She was trying to get somebody to sweep the school of an evening and then come and build the fire of a morning.

So Blanche [sister] and I decided we'd get up earlier and do the milking and then we'd go down and take care of that schoolhouse. And then we would sweep before we went home of an evening.

And we got 5¢ a day for sweeping the schoolhouse and 5¢ for building the fire, so she had a nickel of it and I had a nickel.

Pearl McCall, 89, Daviess County

The teacher was generally required to keep the fire tended and, if there was no janitor, she built the fires, swept floors, washed windows and blackboard, etc. The teachers furnished soap, towels, washbasin and first aid equipment.

The floors were made of wood, and they were oiled twice a year to keep the dust down. They were hard on clothing when playing marbles.

Essie Rumble, 77, Gibson County

Another difference is that we didn't have modern conveniences. When it was dark, we couldn't read and do a lot of things that we can do now with electric lights. Instead, we would have ciphering matches or spelling bees or some kind of contest so that we could continue to learn.

Blanche Burnett, 77, Morgan County

We had a trustee in our school that was a pretty well-to-do man for those times. He said that if the advisory board would buy a globe of the world, he would buy a dictionary. So he bought us that big dictionary for the new schoolhouse. They put that dictionary on a stand back by the door and put a chain on it and fastened it to the floor. And that was one of the outstanding things, because people came from different schools to see those things, because they didn't have them.

Alvah Watson, 97, Allen County

It was the greatest thing when I went to school to stand and salute the flag. We never opened school without singing some patriotic song, and that brought it to your heart and to your life.

Audrey Blackburn, 86, Posey County

We had to be at school at 8:30 and we had a recess in the morning and an hour at noon and a recess in the afternoon.

We went to a one-room school, had one teacher and he taught all eight grades. We had reading, writing, arithmetic, geography, physiology, language, history, and spelling. We had physiology and geography on alternate days, because we couldn't get them all in every day.

Grace Elrod, 86, Jasper County

All eight grades had every subject every day, so the longest you got to dwell on any subject was maybe ten minutes. You'd get up—they called it a recitation then—and they'd set up in front of the teacher's

Iron desks with inkwells for dipping girls'
pigtails and blackboards and maps on the
walls mark a typical schoolroom.
This appears to be a graded school,
with two grades in the room.
Submitted by Rush County

desk on a big long bench. At the beginning of the day she taught the first grade and then she would give them tomorrow's assignment and then second grade and third grade and so on. The rest of the children heard all the grades recite.

There was seven in my class—it was the biggest—and the recitation bench would only hold six, so the seventh child had to set on the front seat of the row of seats. There were five boys and two girls and neither girl wanted to set by a boy. So it was a big race for me and my girl friend Ethel Lee Hoss. It was a big race when she would call our class to see which one of us would have to set by a boy.

Mary Ann Hoskins, Grant County

We had the primer. Before they ever got in the first grade, we has the primer. And they just had a chart for those little ones, and they'd bring the chart out and they'd have a picture of a pig on there. The teacher would ask what that was. Of course, they all knew, but one of them would say "pig" and another would say "hog." Then they'd turn another page, and maybe there'd be a boy and he had a name. And like that.

Pearl McCall, 89, Daviess County

Did they have report cards then?

Oh, yes, but they were grades a little different then. They used "S" for satisfactory and they used "E" for excellent and "G" for good and "P" for poor and "F" for failing.

Thelma Nixon, 68, Union County

I tell you, you had to write. You had copy books, and you had to write. And you had to read. If you stood up to read and you didn't do it right, the teacher would help you by correcting you.

Audry Blackburn, 86, Posey County

Did your teacher stress handwriting when you were going to school?

Yes, we always had writing, from the first to the eighth grade. That's one of the weak points of the schools right now.

Bernice Hirst, 87, Lagrange County

The whole of Hamilton County only had one music teacher in those days. His name was Charlie Carter and he played a violin. He taught all the schools and went from school to school. You could count on him being there one or two days a week. That man would put your major and minor scales on the blackboard, and he'd walk up and down that aisle, sawing that violin, teaching you to sing parts.

I thought it was great. I learned to read music that way. I've never had another music lesson in my life but I can read the treble and bass clef.

Beulah Grinstead, 68, Hamilton County

When I got up in the grades, we had a very strong music department.

I know we put on several very nice operettas when I was a child growing up.

Bernice Hirst, 87, Lagrange County

I liked to make words rhyme, so I wrote poetry. I'd write poetry
about every kid in school. I liked to draw pictures, too, and paint pictures. I liked art in every way. My teacher took my first poem when I
was twelve years old and put it in the LAGRO PRESS. When it was
published, my, I was proud.

Clara Nichols, 79, Wabash County

The first school I went to was a little school, with only 24 in the
school and it was all eight grades. I remember when I was just a child,
there was one of the boys in the eighth grade whose grandfather
worked in a drugstore. He had a box of crayons, and that was the biggest attraction for me that I ever remember.

Elma Matthew, 74, Madison County

Your artist work has always been a part of your life?
My main interest. I didn't have an art teacher in the grades, but on
Friday afternoon we usually had something special, if we had our work
done through the week. It was a one-room school and Miss Brown was
our teacher and she would have a drawing lesson on Friday afternoon.

Beulah Mardis, 76, Johnson County

There was only three in our class. When we would get through with
our work the teacher had assigned to us, we got to go pick up our little
red chairs and go sit in front of the big kids.

It was the biggest thrill for me for her [teacher] to pull down the
maps like a window shade and point out the places. To this day I love
maps.

Opal Gallagher, 72, Shelby County

I loved the upper classes and learned more from them than from my
own class. I found the eighth grade geography fascinating and wanted
to join the class each day. I was allowed to sit with them occasionally
and learned to keep silent, which was hard for a small child, unless
called upon.

Beu Shuel, 74, Gibson County

You wouldn't believe how much we learned from listening to the
older children recite. We were ahead of our time, in a way, because we
were learning what they learned at the same time. Every Friday was a

spelling bee or a cipher match. A cipher match is [with] numbers, and we had this almost every Friday. If you were a third grader you could spell again an eighth grader.

Beulah Grinstead, 68, Hamilton County

This little girl poses in front of a woodpile.
As soon as she changes her school clothes
for everyday clothes,
she will carry in the wood.
Submitted by Miami County

Would you like to go back to one-room teaching again?

It was good. What we learned, we learned. I can still remember learning the multiplication tables. Rote [learning] and listening to the other children was a good review for all of us.

Ilo Coffing, 76, Cass County

Do you think you got as good an education then as they do now?

Well, really, I think we knew basics better when we graduated out of the eighth grade than the seniors do now. And I think the seniors then were equal to college graduates.

Zada McMillan, 79, Grant County

The teacher wasn't the only one who taught in a one-room school. Children taught other children a great many things. The older classes were reciting in the hearing of the lower grades and so many of the memory things, like spelling and multiplication tables, were often learned by the children listening to the older children.

Blanche Burnett, 77, Morgan County

Right across the road from the home in which we are now living stands the remains of an old one-room country school called Scudder School #2 of Beale Township, right over the front door. My grandfather went to school there, my father walked right across the road to go to school there and I walked around the corner to go to school there.

I came to Scudder School and I think at that time the school had been condemned for like 30 years, because it was in relatively poor condition. Then a couple of years after I got into high school, they did some consolidating in the township and built a new Beale School.

It's just kind of special to think that I was one of the last people, maybe even in America, that got to go to an old one-room school with a pot-bellied stove in the middle. It just kind of has its special place.

I think sometimes that the children in our community would be better off to have this influence. If you didn't get it in one grade—if you missed it in the fourth grade—then you could go back and hear the same teacher give the same lesson for two, three, or four years. By the time you got done, you would learn. So maybe there is a lot to be said for the old one-room school.

Jane Gillooly, 37, Daviess County

ATTENDANCE

You mentioned once that you had 11 students in your [whole] school.
There was never more than 12.

Were there all eight grades?
We never had all eight grades, but if there had been a child for each grade, we would have had. School was only for six months.

When did it start?
It started in October. It was out real early, because kids had to work

on the farm. As soon as they could plow, they had to be at home.
Beulah Mardis, 76, Johnson County

We had little children, probably only 20, maybe 25, in the fall to start with. Then in December the crowd began to fill in. The boys come in off the farm. They had hired to be a farmer for six or eight months, but they'd be in school in December, January and February. Then in March they'd drop out and go back to the farm.

So during those months we'd have quite a little rowdiness in school much of the time. They had to put benches in sometimes to make room for all these larger boys.

And now, looking back and thinking about it, I'm not sure the boys came to learn very much. I think they just wanted to get away from home.
Alvah Watson, 97, Allen County

We stayed home in the fall to work until the crops were in. We missed lots of school that way. And after I got big enough to use the washboard I lots of time stayed home on wash day, because with that big a family, there was lots of washing. Mother couldn't have got it all done. So lots of time I had to stay home on wash day.
Were you treated any different for it, at school?
Oh, no, this was customary. The big girls helped out at home, just like the big boys did.
Edna Winter, 74, Pulaski County

I used to help shock wheat when I was a kid. We used to raise a lot of sorghum, and you would have to strip that. It was bad, because it always come in September when the kids were all in school and then Mom and Dad [would do it] or sometimes Dad would hire some people that would help.
Rather than keeping you out of school?
Oh, yes. We didn't hardly ever have to stay home to work. A lot of children did have to, but Dad and Mom never were like that. They sent us to school. We were very fortunate. A lot of people my age, never even got to go to high school.
Thelma Roehr, 69, Posey County

I always enjoyed school. A lot of kids don't want to go, but I was mad when I was sick and couldn't go.
Alfreda Wesner, 47, White County

DISCIPLINE

I always liked my teacher, except one. She was part Indian and she would hold that threat over our heads. If we didn't behave ourselves, she was going to scalp us and hang our scalp out in the hall. And I thought she'd do it (laughter).

You were convinced?

I could just see my scalp hanging out there.

Eula Kelso, 78, Lawrence County

Did they have discipline problems in school?

Yes; now the teachers in our school, the men teachers got $1.85 per day and the women got $1.75. There was ten cents difference and they would make sure to send a man teacher where they thought they needed it.

They had a place on the blackboard where they'd lay a whip, and that was just a warning to the children.

We had two teachers and one of them was pretty severe. In fact, he got so bad the parents had to let him go, but he was the one they had with the big boys.

But our lady teacher, she had different ways of punishing children. She would draw a ring on the blackboard and you would have to put your nose in it. Or I have been tied to her apron strings and she'd walk back and forth across the room, and you would tag along just like a little dog with a rope on. And she had different ways of embarrassing you. One time we had to spell and if you misspelled the word "wood," for instance, she'd make you go carry in the wood.

Alvah Watson, 97, Allen County

A Miss Cope was my first teacher. You would have to mind her— what she said. We had big seats, and two of us could sit there, but she put a big piece of firewood between us, and she said, "Now if you whisper, I'll tie this handkerchief so tight around your head that you can't whisper." After we got so big, they didn't tie the handkerchief around our heads. Then, if we whispered, we had to stand up in front.

Flossie Foster, 95, Hendricks County

One time I waited on my friend and we came in school late. Well, our teacher he met us in the hallway. He got us by the hair of the head, and he cracked our heads together and I thought I saw stars in the daytime.

So I went home and I asked my mother, did she ever see stars in the daytime, and I told her what had happened. She said, "Well, now, let that be a lesson to you." Well, it was, because I had a lump on my head. You know, that learnt me never to be late anymore.

Those days the teacher could lick the kids. They could do about anything and get by with it.

Masa Scheerer, 82, Huntington County

The older ones used to play pranks on the teacher. Teachers always treated the kids. They always got candy and had a treat. This one teacher, he wasn't gonna treat and the big boys, they put a pole across the road when school was out and they wouldn't let him go till he said he would bring treats the next morning.

So he brought the treats.

Mable Wingate, 89, Blackford County

The bigger boys would get mischievous and they would take the girls' hair and stick it in the little ink wells, a little hole where you got your ink out of. Sometimes people would write notes and throw them across to people and then the teacher would hit you and make you read the note [aloud], and then they would stand them in the corner with a dunce cap.

And then the boys would put frogs in the teacher's desk. There was a little drawer in the desk and sometimes she would open that and out would jump the frog.

Frances Harley, 89, Marshall County

We had a teacher some of the bigger boys didn't like. One day, one of them brought some sorghum molasses to school. She had a habit of pulling her chair under her desk when she left the room, and she seldom ever looked when she pulled it out to sit down. So while she was out on the playground, they poured sorghum molasses on the seat of her chair.

She didn't look and she sat down in it. Was that woman mad! She knew right away who did it. So she told them to go out to the playground and get a switch off the tree out there. Now they brought the switch, but they cut little notches in it, so when she went to switch them, it flew apart. It broke up.

Did that make her more angry?

Worse than ever. She laughed about it later, but at the time it really upset her. She made them stay in after school until she got ready to go home and then she sent notes home to the parents for them to come to school next day. And they did. Those three boys were always doing something.

Pearl Sollars, 70, Tippecanoe County

Do you think the students in general were more serious then, or about the same as now?

I don't think we dared be otherwise. We weren't all smart, and we didn't always study, but we didn't sass a teacher, and we pretended to study, if we didn't.

Beulah Mardis, 76, Johnson County

TEACHERS

I did not go to the first grade, because my dad had taught school and he started teaching all of us kids, I guess as soon as we got big enough to walk—maybe even a little before that. He was never much of a phonics teacher, so when I got to school in the second grade, the other kids knew that and I had to catch up on that.

Alice Jones, 74, Kosciusko County

My uncle, my dad's brother, was a schoolteacher at school several years while I was going there. He had a son my age and he was smart as he could be, and I just had to work myself to death to try to keep up with him. And my uncle, he would get aggravated at the other kids, he would always punish Gary and me.

Cleo Borders, 75, Martin County

I come from a family of teachers. I never had my own mother as a teacher, but I had the woman who became my mother-in-law for my first grade teacher. She taught in the Frankton system for almost 40 years. She taught long enough to have my first two children as her students.

I had my dad as a teacher, as well as my principal, as a seventh grader and as a senior. I had him for civics as a senior, and he taught an English class when I was in the seventh grade. I remember what a hurdle it was for me—I didn't know what to call him when I was in the seventh and he was my teacher. I didn't want to say "Mr. Copeland," and I thought it was undignified to say "Daddy."

Did he cross examine you at home?

No, not too much. I do remember one time when I was in junior high. We had citizenship grades then, and the girl I sat with in study hall and I giggled so much that I came home with a D in deportment. I got a real talking to at home, but then I got called to the principal's office, and the principal was my dad. My dad was the principal in his office, he wasn't my dad. I'll never forget going to the principal's office. He told me, "Young lady, don't you ever bring home a grade like that again."

Loranelle Kimmerling, 54, Madison County

A teacher, almost indistinguishable by size or age, poses to the right of her group of scholars.
Submitted by Jasper County

My mother would never go to school with me. She thought she wasn't smart enough to talk to a schoolteacher, since she was born of farm folks.

Burnetha Knox, 68, St. Joseph County

I had a man teacher that was related to my father and one day I had to raise my hand to leave the room, and he ignored me. He wouldn't let me go. I went home and told my dad that he wouldn't let me leave the room. Dad said, "Next time that happens, you get up and leave the room. If there is anything said about it, you send him to me."

Alma Knecht, 78, Wabash County

I went to school in six different schools in the eight years that I went to school, so I was thoroughly disgusted by that time. [Changing schools so much was hard] and by that time I didn't have any desire at all to go to high school.

This teacher at Catlin School never liked me. She treated me kind of bad, because we never had much. It was cold that winter and you know we only had those big old round pot-bellied stoves settin' in the school. I had to sit over next to the window—on the north side next to the window. I was sitting over there in a short-sleeved dress, and I was about to freeze and I wanted to go over and sit by the stove.

She said, "Well, if you'd dress warmer, you wouldn't get so cold." But I didn't even own anything to dress any warmer. I didn't own a sweater to my name. But she never cared for me, and that's the way she did me.

Laura Drake, 77, Parke County

We had all kinds of teachers; some of them good and some of them indifferent. But some of us youngsters were good and some of us weren't.

Margaret Butler, 87, Steuben County

Our teacher drove a horse pulling a buggy. The big boys would help her remove the harness and put her horse in a little shed beside the coal house and they would feed it. When school was over, they helped her harness the horse up again and she was ready to go home.

Gee, it sure was fun to spend the night with your teacher. I was lucky to get to spend the night twice in one year.

Marjorie Malott, 67, Pike County

The teacher took turns staying at the pupils' homes many times. That was the regular place for her to stay. Two of the men that taught lived right in the neighborhood, but if there was an outside teacher, there was always a place for them to stay.

Iva Crouse, 85, White County

We used to love our teachers. We had a teacher, one time, who used to stay at our house sometimes. And we had lots of respect for the teachers.

The children took them things from the farm. I don't know whether they did that in the city or not, but we used to take things. Maybe we'd get a quart of berries, or we'd go out and get some apples and we'd take some, or maybe we'd have a taffy pull and maybe we'd take the teacher some. Because she was special, very special.

Teachers in a one-room schoolhouse was faced with many problems, far too many. Pay was small, but still more than the average, for money was hard to come by during my childhood days.

But love and respect was worth more than the bank account. One teacher we had for three years was a wonderful, kind person. She never knew, I'm sure, the influence she had on the lives of the children. One of the sad days of our school was the day she said goodbye, for she was appointed to another school.

Alvah Watson, 97, Allen County

Who do you remember looking up to as you were growing up?

Mostly schoolteachers. They were my biggest idol, because we always looked up to them and they were highly respected in the community.

I remember my first grade teacher. I thought she was wonderful. And I had two English teachers in high school that I thought were the most wonderful people on earth. You always had to measure up in their classes.

Betty Alvey, 60, Howard County

I had one teacher in common school that left an influence greater than anybody in my life, apart from my family. He was the greatest man that I ever knew when I was growing up. Everything in school, he made it beautiful and meaningful. We had a lot of poetry in reading and he made every line real. You can make your life count in this world. He just inspired you every day in school to make your life count the most that day.

Do you think he affected the other school kids the same way?

No. There were three girls my age and we three girls went through school together, but they never expressed anything about him like I did. I talked to Lottie Furlong once about him, and she said "I don't even remember any of that."

But if teachers could realize the privilege they have of putting something in children's hearts. Maybe I was the only one that he left all that, but he sure did leave it with me. He was something to me, and I can just never be grateful enough for him. He made life so beautiful and so meaningful. It was just wonderful.

Audry Blackburn, 86, Posey County

GETTING
TO SCHOOL

It didn't matter whether it was raining or snowing or what, we went to school. I don't know that I ever missed a day on account of weather. I was always at school. I can remember wading snowdrifts and missing the road and going out in the fields to get around drifts I couldn't wade because it was too deep, but I would get to school.
Margaret Butler, 87, Steuben County

I had to walk a mile and a half to school and one year I never was tardy a minute or missed a day.
Alice Potts, 81, Newton County

I walked by myself two and a half miles from my home to St. Joseph school for the first year. It was dark when I left in the morning and dark when I went home.
Otillia Buehler, 90, Dubois County

We walked to school, if the river wasn't over the road. Part of the time we went in the boat. And sometimes it was so muddy. My sister and I was going to school on that same road, and she was small and she got hung up in the mud and I couldn't get her out. I had to go get a cousin to come help me get her out of the mud.
Catherine Summers, 67, Harrison County

We walked to school and we walked fast in order to get to school in time to play a long time before school started. We walked so fast I just had to go on a jog trot. And then when our younger sister started, we were walking fast and she had to just sort of dog trot to keep up with us. Mother and Aunt Mary always said they felt sorry for the little child.
Erma Agnew, 88, Decatur County

I always remember the walk to school and going past a creek in Wyatt and we'd watch the frogs in spring and water glistening. To me, [those are] some of the nice things of life to remember.
Helen Marker, 66, St. Joseph County

When I was old enough, I walked to school with neighbor children.

We had to cross the railroad over to the Edge Water School, and when the water came up, it would go across the road so deep that we couldn't get across. My father had a mule that he fox-hunted with, and he would put me in the saddle and go with me to the edge of the water. I would ride to the railroad, get off, put the reins around the saddle horn, and the mule would go back to him on the other side of the water. Then, when the water got too deep for her and he felt like he didn't want me to go through it anymore, he would take me across in a boat. Then the water would get so high that they would have to close the school down. This was backwater, from the Wabash River.

Vernell Saltzman, 81, Posey County

The winter which was my second year in school, we had a very large snow. When Maurice and I started to school that morning we met our cousins, Grace, Willis and Marjorie Scholl.

The snowdrifts were so deep that we smaller ones could hardly make it over the snow, or through the snow. So Maurice took the lead, then Marjorie, Grace, Willis and then myself.

When we got there, we were the only people there, besides the teacher, so she sent us home a half hour later. Then we still had to make a new path because it was snowing and blowing so bad.

Harriett Gwinnup, 73, Fayette County

I remember the big snowstorm, I think it was in 1918, and when they began to let us start to school again, my sister and I walked right over the top of the rail fences. We would go every day, walking over the top of the fences. I would say drifts were four or five feet high over the fences, and they would bear our weight.

Ruth Grover, 79, Wells County

It seems to me that snow used to pile up lots more than it does now. I suppose those old rail fences caused that. We had only half a mile to go to school, but it would just blow the road full, and Dad would lay those fence rails down between the fields and take us to school in the bobsled. But he'd have to go out in the fields a long way around to get around the snow banks.

Maggie Owen, 95, Whitley County

Our hired man usually got the horse ready for us in the morning, and all hitched up. Then we had a full mile and half drive. We went every day we could get through. We got to Mt. Carmel, had to unhitch the horse and put her in the stall and take the bridle off and put a halter on her. Then at noon we had to go down and feed her.

When the snow was on, we'd sometimes go in the sleigh. Sometimes we'd go in the sleigh and we had to come home in the mud—the snow had warmed and melted enough that it wasn't a very enjoyable trip.

One winter—in 1918, I believe—I couldn't get home, so I stayed with my aunt for a whole week. We couldn't get through the drifts, but we had school just the same.

Hazel Williams, 79, Franklin County

We had two miles to go to school. The bigger ones did walk, but they was so many of us a-going and the little ones [had trouble walking], so Dad got permission of the trustee to build a little barn or little stable. He let us drive the horse and buggy to school. And we put our little horse in that little stable, and we drove back and forth to school.

It got pretty cold in the wintertime. I know a couple of times I had frozen feet. We used to heat bricks and put them in the buggy to set our feet on, but still your feet got so cold they would freeze.

Cora Keplinger, 80, Huntington County

When my brother got old enough to drive, we drove the horse and buggy. He put the horse down in my Uncle Dave's barn. Brother would go down at noon to feed the horse. My father furnished the feed for our horse and Uncle Dave's horse.

We had a horse that had been a racer at one time. We called him Bill. On the way home from school, sometimes there would be another horse and buggy come up in back of us. Bill would just take off and sometimes we'd be going so fast we couldn't make the corner. We would just go straight on until Bill slowed down.

Iva Crouse, 85, White County

We had more fun when we was going to school. If it would be bad weather, my mom would hitch up the horse and come over and get my brother, sister and I, and we brought our two cousins along home.

We were all in the buggy, and it was muddy as all get out, and when we went by, some of the kids throwed stones at the horse and hit it. So away we went, just a-sailin', and we had to go over the railroad track, and a train was coming.

My mom tried to slow the horse down, to let the train go by, but that horse, she couldn't hold him. She'd keep a-sayin' "Whoa, Jimmy! Whoa, Jimmy!" and us kids was all hollering and laughing. We just went over the railroad track a-bouncin' and the train went by.

And Mom says, "I'll never come after you any more." She says, "Just walk home, it's only 2½ mile." So after that, we always had to walk home.

Masa Scheerer, 82, Huntington County

When I was 17 years old I drove the school bus. Started at Christmastime the year I was 17 and I drove two and half years. Drove a horse bus. And manys the time, in the spring when we had what we called the "spring thaw-out" and the bottom would go out of the road, I'd take my kids within a half mile of school, tie my horses to a fence post and walk the kids to school. Then in the evening, I tied my horses

The children of Ira Ely, Wakarusa,
Indiana, getting into their school bus.
J. C. Allen Collection

at this corner and I walked down and led my kids out. I think I had 16 or 17 on the bus. And I drove that bus two and a half years for the whole sum of four or five dollars a week. But that was a lot of money you know.

And, by the way, the heat in that school bus was a wood stove that was under the bus. You got out and fired it up. The wood came off the wood pile at home. Occasionally they would have coal at the schoolhouse and I would go and get a bucket of coal in really bad weather.

I loved being out with the horses. If Dad was home I could put the team in the barn and unharness it when I got home in the morning.

But if he wasn't going to be home to get me started in the evening, I had to leave the harness on my horses all day.

Edna Winter, 74, Pulaski County

We had a horse hack with seats along the side that looked like a stagecoach. It had one seat in the middle without a back. One time the roads were icy and we were getting pretty close to the school building. One of the horses slipped and fell and broke a leg. We children walked the rest of the way to school. At that time they didn't know how to care for it, so as soon as anything broke a leg, they just shot it.

And we heard them shoot it before we got to the school building. That always bothered me. I couldn't stand to see things like that done.

Pearl Sollars, 70, Tippecanoe County

We had horse-driven hacks to take us to school, and they would heat them with a heater. You know, that heater would get hot enough that we would pop corn on it.

Phyllis Frank, 79, DeKalb County

They had a horsedriven hack, but we didn't go on it because there weren't enough youngsters to have a hack. The trustee hired my father to take us and another family of children to school. We had a carriage at that time, and we took the other youngsters to school with us.

Thelma Robeson, 72, Fayette County

At that time we went to school in a hack. They drove horses to it. It was a closed-in vehicle that had a little tiny stove in it that they heated up for us.

We lived on a side road and it was so bad one spring that the driver would stop at his mother's place and he would unhitch the two horses from this hack and hitch them to a buggy and then come up the side road and pick my sister and I up and take us down to that hack, and then get in and finish the route. But the mud was almost axle deep in the buggy and he couldn't come up that road with that hack—he'd mire down.

Laura Drake, 72, Parke County

One time in 1918 there was such a bad snow and the hack driver put a wagon box on a bobsled and put straw in the bottom and put a blanket over that and had a canvas on top. We crawled in the back end and sat down flat on the seat.

Lois Wagoner, 76, Fulton County

By the time the hack wound around the different homes where they picked up the children, it would be eleven miles one way. That was quite a long way with horses. My mother would take me to the road by lantern light, where I met the hack, and meet me there with the lantern in the evening. The school hours were 8:30 in the morning to 4:00 in the evening plus the hack ride. I wonder what children would say now if they had to attend school that long.

Mary Graver, 80, Wayne County

My father drove horses to a deluxe kid hack. He drove a beautiful white team. The hack was closed with side and rear curtains and a storm front. It also had a coal stove. Sometimes children brought corn and popped it.

A few times I went with my father when the weather was good, and I believe those trips were equal to my first airplane trip.

Essie Rumble, 77, Gibson County

When my sister was young, she road a horse-drawn hack. By the time I was six years old, I remember the old bus. It was motor driven.

A lot of people in town were afraid of buses. When our children were growing up, they had to go on the bus. People would say "Aren't you afraid for them to ride a bus?"

Eleanor Cheek, 61, Union County

We had a horse-drawn hack until I was a freshman and then we got a motor bus. This bus had to bring us in from the north and we waited in the assembly room under the supervision of a high school teacher while the same driver and bus went out west of town and picked up a load. In the evening it was the same thing. We waited until he took the children west.

Alice Guyer, 68, Wabash County

The school bus wasn't like they are today. The school bus driver had no connection with the kids. It was just sitting on the back of the truck. You got in the back, and the seats were long-ways. They heated it with the exhaust—you could lean down and see the red exhaust pipe—and it was very good to burn shoes. Get in with cold feet and warm then, and it wasn't a little bit till you had your shoe soles ruined.

How many did it haul?

About 20 to 25. If there were too many, the boys would stand on the back step and ride on the outside.

Marie Weber, 71, Rush County

SCHOOL
CLOTHES

I remember particularly that girls all wore aprons to school over their dresses. That was because a wool dress was what we had to wear in the wintertime, and they couldn't be washed like the wash dresses now. You had to wear an apron to keep your dress clean so you could wear your dress to school most of the winter. We wore long black stockings and long underwear, because we had to wade through the snow.

Harriet Gwinnup, 73, Fayette County

We'd go to school with a school dress, and we'd wear it all week. But we wouldn't wear it when we came home. We'd always change our clothes, from the inside out. But you'd wear the same dress the next day.

Bessie Werner, 80, Pulaski County

Do you remember what your dresses were like?
Oh, they were long, down about my ankles and my mother made them, of course.
Did you hand down clothes?
Oh, yes, we never disposed of anything. You used it some way.
Do you remember the colors of your dresses?
My father was a Quaker, and he didn't like to see my mother or me have anything red. It was always blue or gray or black. A little brown. Usually blue.
Could you have prints?
Oh, yes. The prints were nice. Plaids, too.

Pearl Garrison, 92, Carroll County

I had two school dresses and one Sunday dress. Every Saturday we had to wash them. We had to take our school shoes off every evening to do our chores. And we had a pair of Sunday shoes.

Rosalia Mehringer, 79, Dubois County

What about your shoes?
They was high top shoes, but no buttons, I always had ties—shoe laces.

Did you have boots?
Well, we called them overshoes. They had buckles on them.
Alma Smith, 73, Grant County

In cold weather, we all got mighty cold. Some children didn't have
overshoes and their feet would be wet when they got there. The teacher
would let us pull seats up close to the stove. We'd take turns sitting
there and drying and getting warm. Then we'd go back and let someone else take it.
Nellie Frakes, 71, Perry County

Walking to school through the woods.
Notice the lunch boxes and the books
held together with a book strap.
J. C. Allen Collection

We always walked to school over dirt roads. The road had a bank
on either side, and we would get up on that bank and walk to keep
from getting in the mud.
Until I finished common school, my mother knitted all the stockings
for the entire family.
I had these long black stockings and that mud would get all over
them. We would sit before this pot-bellied stove at school and we
would try to scape that mud off.
Audry Blackburn, 86, Posey County

We wore long socks and long underwear with a strap under our feet to hold that underwear down.

Eula Kelso, 78, Lawrence County

I lived a mile from school and I had to walk. And I think the thing I hated most about cold weather was that I had to wear long underwear. It was woolen underwear, and it itched. We wore long lisle stockings [over it] and I would get to school and run to the bathroom and roll my stockings down and roll my underwear up and then roll my hose back up. I didn't want those wrinkles [from the underwear] showing on my legs. We all did it, because we were so embarrassed. We'd set around with great big rolls around our thighs.

Then when we'd get ready to go home, why we'd go in again. My aunt was the teacher at the time, and she said she had to have a special recess for the girls to go to the bathroom and get their hose back in position to walk home (laughter).

Did your mother know this?

Oh, yes, she was aware of everything that went on at school, because my aunt went home and tattled (laughter).

Jean Brechbill, 65, DeKalb County

Hair was long and braided except for special occasions, when Mother did the hair up on rags to make long curls, ornamented by large ribbons.

Essie Rumble, 77, Gibson County

I had my pigtails put in ink wells many times, but I also had one cut off.

Mother parted my hair in the middle and she thought she had to braid it so tight it would look like when I got home at night, it would look like when I left of mornings. She would have it so tight I would have a headache. I would plead with her not to get it so tight, but she thought she had to, to get it to stay up.

So one morning my brother felt sorry for me. Before we ever went to school, he went out the front door with a pair of scissors and I went out the back door and he cut a pigtail off, the one that was hurting the worst. We went on to school, and Mother didn't know until I came home that evening with only one pigtail.

Boy, was she mad! I said, "I asked you not to braid them so tight. I can't stand it." She said, "Earl, why did you cut that?" "'Cause I know how it hurt." So she had to cut the other pigtail. That way I got my hair cut, but it wasn't too pleasant for a little while.

Pearl Sollars, 70, Tippecanoe County

I remember my folks cut my hair for a while, but when we got up to a certain age, we'd go to the barber shop. They would put this board across the arms of the chair to make you higher, and set you up there like the men.

They [parents] would always say, "Trim her bangs and cut her hair on the sides until the tips of her ears show, and shingled up the back." We did that when we were going to get our pictures taken or something like that. It was an occasion.

Going to the barber shop with the stove in the corner was a good place to hear everything.

Evelyn Rigsby, 58, Madison County

FOOD
AT SCHOOL

I would start to school in the morning on a well-filled stomach with pancakes, maple syrup, sausage and sometimes sauerkraut.

Lucille Imes, 82, Noble County

To get to school on time we arose at four o'clock in the morning. We children helped Mother prepare breakfast, which was a huge meal consisting of meat, gravy, oats, apple butter, biscuits, milk and coffee.

My sister and I washed dishes, while my mother prepared our lunches, which we carried to school in small buckets.

Violet David, 79, Brown County

I remember walking to school in the winter. There were persimmon trees on the path. We would stop and get frozen persimmons and eat them.

Juanita Harden, 49, Bartholomew County

There were six of us in school at one time. The girls would have the kitchen table cleaned up and the breakfast dishes done and those lunch pails out, and they would be packing lunches.

What did you have in a lunch pail, then?

Bread and jelly, or peanut butter. We seldom took meat sandwiches.

My mother was always afraid of food poisoning, so we didn't take lunch meats. We did have—and some people think this is terrible—we had bean sandwiches. And we loved them. She'd put a little butter on the bread and then mash up and spread on beans. We called them soup beans—navy beans, lots of people call them. Mash those up, spread it on; put on a little extra salt and pepper and the top slice of bread, and we thought they were delicious. I like them yet to this day, but my four children turn their nose up at them.

The one thing I hated was apple butter. That soaked in the bread. 'Course, my mother baked all the bread. We didn't have bread from the bakery like we do now.

We had popcorn, so sometimes we would have a popcorn ball in our lunch. Not too much baked goods. I think, with eight children, it was just too hard to keep it on hand. You couldn't hardly stash enough away for lunches.

Mildred Weaver, 64, Pulaski County

We raised most of what we took. In the summer if we didn't get the beans when they were green, we let them ripen and dry, then we shelled them out and had dried beans. It never failed. If we had a pot of beans one night during the week, that was our school lunch the next day, a glass of cold dried beans. I told the children they were good, but they couldn't think so. And then we took a lot of cold sweet potatoes to school. Butter them and eat them that way.

Hazel Williams, 79, Franklin County

What did you take in your lunch?
The thing that stands out in my mind was I'd have egg sandwiches. She [Mother] always made hot biscuits every morning for breakfast. We had hot biscuits and rice and she'd fry eggs. She'd make me a sandwich out of the eggs and those biscuits. And I just loved them.

Laura Drake, 72, Parke County

We'd take boiled eggs in the wintertime and some of that salty old ham.

Alice Potts, 81, Newton County

She would make me a meat sandwich and then a jellybread sandwich and a banana or an orange, and milk.
Did you take your own milk?
Yes.

Gaby Moon, 69, Clay County

We had tenderloin sandwiches and ham sandwiches, and, oh, we had fine food to take to school and enjoyed it.

Mary Summers, 69, Newton County

We carried our dinner bucket, a little old gallon molasses bucket, with our lunch in it. All homecooked food, none of it was bought. Whatever we had. Sausage, or ham—all home-cured meat—we'd take our sandwiches and we'd have cookies that Mother baked and that was our lunch. Oh, and an apple, we always had an apple that was raised at home.

Did you ever trade any of your lunch off with others?

I didn't, but my brother was awful bad about that. He'd always trade off his bananas and sometimes he'd get a fried potato sandwich.

Opal Whitsett, 84, Scott County

A school lunch supplemental program, with milk in glass bottles and a sandwich furnished by an Extension Homemakers club program.
Submitted by Purdue University

What kind of lunches did you have for school?

Well, we had to fix our lunches. We didn't have a mother to bake for us. Dad bought lunch meat and cookies. It was during the Depression and a lot of my classmates were having harder times than I was, seemed like. I would trade my boughten cookies or my boughten meat sandwich for something they had from home, because theirs tasted so much better to me, and they thought mine was something great (chuckle). So it worked out real well.

Frances Bennett, 63, Montgomery County

Did you have the hot lunch program back then?

In the bucket you carried (chuckle). Packed your bucket before you left. If you didn't get what you liked to eat, it was your tough luck. Or you traded with somebody. That was the big thing, to trade. If somebody had a boughten bread sandwich [I'd trade] because I was sick and tired of homemade bread. What you'd do now for homemade bread! We had meat about every morning for breakfast, so we could take some of that meat and make a sandwich. And usually homemade jelly.

Dorothy Hoffman, 54, Adams County

I acquired a great dislike for cold sandwiches. I still feel this. I prefer a hot bowl of soup to a sandwich, any day.

Dorothy Kelley, 69, Hendricks County

Our school had three rooms and a basement. But we had a home ec. class. Mary Dell Williams was the home ec teacher. And the home ec teacher managed and planned the hot lunches that they had at noon. The parents would donate and she would see, usually, that they had something like chili or vegetable soup or cocoa or something like that, and the parents would donate the products.

Thelma Nixon, 68, Union County

[We had] wonderful meals. Homemade doughnuts and, oh, the peach cobbler, and homemade chili. They could cook just as good as my mother, I thought.

Judi Merkel, 34, Adams County

I went to Wyman Grade School, and it was right next to Harris Teachers College. The college had a lunch room and we could go over there and eat lunch. It about blows your mind when you think of it today! We could get anything we wanted for a nickel apiece: ice cream, salad, meat and potatoes—a thin slice of beef with a scoop of mashed potatoes and gravy.

For a nickel?

A nickel a scoop.

Julie Huseman, 64, Montgomery County

In high school there was Weilbrenner's Grocery, just one block west. If my dad had enough money, he would give me a little bit of money, like a dime, to buy my lunch at that grocery. This man would make sandwiches for you. He would cut bologna and he had a loaf of bread and he would make you a sandwich. And I would always buy one of those big pickles out of the barrel. You could buy your lunch, a sandwich and a pickle, for a dime.

Thelma Roehr, 69, Posey County

During the Depression, my friend always had a dime every day at school, and she bought an apple and a candy bar. I brought a peanut butter sandwich to school and I ate at school, then I'd take a walk with her and she would go up town and buy her candy bar. I never once thought about asking my mother for a dime, so I could have a candy bar.

Helen Sauser, 64, Wayne County

I grew up in town. We didn't have buses and nobody drove me to school. My kids can't believe I walked that far. It's at least a mile and I walked to school, home for lunch, back again, and home from school.

Donna Marbach, 41, Adams County

The grammar school was approximately six block from my home. We were not allowed to bring a lunch or stay at school. We had to walk home for lunch and then back again in the afternoon. So, regardless of rain, snow, or cold weather, we had to walk to school. The children in the country are a lot better, when they get picked up right outside of their front door, so city people don't have it near as convenient as country people when it comes to school.

Florence DeYoung, 68, Jasper County

I just lived a half a block from school. I'd go home at recess to get something to eat, go home for lunch, too.

Jane White, 78, Owen County

We always carried our dinners in a lunch box or bucket. And ours was a large bucket, with a place on top to carry milk. Of course, Lennie being the older, my mother would always insist that she carry the full bucket because it was heavier. And Lennie would carry it to school, but when we came home I was supposed to help carry it.

She'd start out from school with it, but go a little piece and she'd set it down. She'd done her share; now I had to do it. But I wouldn't pick it up; I'd go on past it. But I knew that bucket had to go on home, so, finally, I'd go back after it.

Of course, I'd get to crying and Lennie'd walk on so independently. I had to carry the bucket home. But she'd take it again when we got almost home, and Mother never knew that I had to do most of the carrying to get it home.

When we'd get home from school, our mother would probably be out doing chores, but before she'd go to the barn, she'd fix a skillet on top of the heating stove with bread and milk. Did you ever eat boiled bread and milk? We thought it was pretty delicious. And that was our supper, too, because we'd eat so much of that that we didn't want anything after.

Erma Agnew, 88, Decatur County

After school we started home with several neighbor children. It would be almost dark when we arrived home, cold and hungry. My mother would be putting supper on the table, and I never smelled anything better.

After the dishes were washed and the chores all done, my father would bring in a crock of apples and my mother would pop corn that we had raised. We would sit around the table on which the coal oil lamp sat. We would study our lessons and eat popcorn and apples.

Violet David, 79, Brown County

PLAY
AT SCHOOL

We had many school activities in those days, but they were different than we have today. There weren't any ball teams or things of that nature. There were just we children at school. We would draw up sides and play. We'd play ball or handy-over. Played different games, like Hide and Seek, things of that kind.

Iva Crouse, 85, White County

The teachers played with the children at recess. Some of the favorite games were Bear; Stink Base; Rover, Rover; Soft Ball; Move Up; Black Man; Anti-Over; Drop the Handkerchief; Crack the Whip; races; spinning tops; marbles; blackboard games. A very popular game was rolling hoops and hoop races. Snow was always welcome, with fox and goose; coasting; snow men; snow angels and snow balling.

Essie Rumble, 77, Gibson County

So many games we played at our school they didn't have at others. Some of them were way, way back, in other times, like Queen Ann Lost Her Bonnet. That one would probably go way back. Another one [was] Here Comes the Duke A-Roving. One man—a boy—would be a duke. And he would dance. "Here comes the duke a-roving, tanscy, tanscy, tee." And we would dance toward him. "What are you roving here for?" And he'd rove here to get married. Then we'd say, "Please take one of us, sir!" and he'd say "You are all too black and rusty." "We're just as good as you are." "The fairest one that I can see is so-and-so, come with me." And then he'd choose a girl and then the next round the girl would choose a boy. Same thing, over and over. Another one handed down, I suppose, was "I want to be a granger, happy as a miller."

Grace Heinzman, 86, Hamilton County

We played Andy Over a lot. Do you know what that is?

Tell me about it. I don't know what Andy Over is.

We would choose sides on each side of the schoolhouse and we would throw the ball over and try to catch it and then run around and catch these people on the other side.

Oh, you threw it over the roof?

Yes, they were little schoolhouses.

Remember if the ball didn't go over what you would yell?

Andy didn't come. But if it went over, whoever caught it. Then we would all run around and try to grab those other kids. Sometimes you would catch them and sometimes you wouldn't.

What if you did?

They had to go on your side then. Tha's the way you increased your team.

We played that, and we always played marbles and jumped the rope. I just loved to jump the rope. I was telling someone the other day about Hot Pepper, and they said, "What in the world is that?" Well, you turned it [jumping rope] as fast as you could go and jumped as fast as you could jump.

Do you remember the little rhymes you jumped to?

I don't believe I can. It's been so long. You would run in and out, and sometimes they would turn backwards, and I don't know what you called that.

Backdoors, I believe. Did you do doubles, too, with two ropes at once.
Oh, yes.

Then we would put on shows ourselves, for the other kids at school. This was at recess, when we were doing our fun.

And there was a big ditch down by the school where I went, and it had willows. We would straddle those willows and swing out over the ditch.

Audry Blackburn, 86, Posey County

A lot of the games we played were connected with running. One of them was Ouch. You'd have the children all line up, hand in hand, and crack the whip. Somebody would say "Ouch!" and the last one would go like this and the little kids on the end would just roll.

Grace Heinzman, 86, Hamilton County

Playground fun on a homemade
merry-go-round.
Submitted by Purdue University

I've studied about this so much [thought about it] and that Razz-Ma-Tazz-Tee, now how would you spell that and how did we play it?

Cleo Borders, 75, Martin County

We used to play Give Us a Wink. There was a space by the big tree at the corner [of the schoolhouse] and you had to go hide. Of course, they run off the school grounds, back in the woods, and then they hid—nobody could find them. You had to find everybody. You had to bring them back to that base. We played and played that. Everytime the teacher caught us back there, he would go and ring his bell, and we would all have to come home safe.

And we used to play that game with a tin can. We used to hit it with a stick. It was the most dangerous game. Everybody had a stick and you hit one can and the idea was to hit the can to your goal line.

Thelma Roehr, 69, Posey County

We had a big tree out by the schoolhouse and the kids would pull the limbs down and we'd get hold of them and we'd get a good grip and then they'd let that limb go and you'd go way up in the air.

I remember one time I didn't get a good grip and I got way up in the air and I fell and hit the back of my head.

I didn't want to tell anybody and we always had to go up on the big recitation bench up front. She [teacher] called the spelling class up that afternoon, and I couldn't see the board. I couldn't write, I couldn't see, and I started crying. She wanted to know what was the matter and the kids told her. Well, that was the end of the tree swinging.

Mary Sheeks, 73, Lawrence County

At grade school we had tar roofs. Us kids would go out behind the school building when it was hot and we would pull tar off the roof and chew it. We would have a ball chewing tar.

Did you have any ill effects?

We never swallowed. When the bell rang we would go in and we would spit it out. I have often wondered why that roof didn't leak. There were so many of us doing it.

Pearl Sollars, 70, Tippecanoe County

My first grade teacher was very strict and I was frightened to death. Marie Shields was in the eighth grade, and at noon and recess I took her hand and stood there until school took up. I was so frightened.

Juanita Hunter, 81, Scott County

We had a teacher, Mr. Munchel, and one thing he made us do, we always had to play together, boys and girls, everybody had to play together. We couldn't be separated, which we didn't like too much. The girls would rather play with the girls and not with the boys, too.

Martha Werner, 63, Franklin County

Our school was on a little knoll and at the south side a little down hill, there were two or three real big trees. That was where the girls played. We played London Bridge is Falling Down over and over. We played a game called Mother, the Teakettle's Boiling Over. I don't remember how it was played, but I think there was an old witch in it. When there was snow on the ground often the boys and girls would play Fox and Geese together, but usually the boys preferred to play ball.

Ruth Snyder, 83, Marshall County

I can remember, by being in a rural school, in the fall of the year or in the spring of the year, we would pick wild flowers in the nearby woods at recess. Those kinds of things you can do when you're in a rural school.

The softball game at recess—everybody played—whether you were good or mediocre. Everybody played, because we needed everybody to make up a team.

Judi Merkel, 34, Adams County

Was your baseball and your bat bought at a store?
Oh, no. Well, they'd go out in the woods and cut off a big limb, and hew it down so that we could grip it [for a bat] or else they'd take a board and make a bat. They would take and unravel socks and wrap that yarn around something hard and that was our ball that we played with.

Alice Potts, 81, Newton County

At recess we always had such a good time. We would go skating and we would get out on our sleds. We had such a good time.

Cleo Borders, 75, Martin County

In the wintertime they would throw snowballs and some of them would pump water and made snowballs so they were like ice. The teacher got after them and made them quit, because they would hurt.

Francis Harley, 89, Marshall County

The schoolhouse was on a hill, and we'd take our sled in the winter and slide up and down.
That would be fun, with just a few of you.
Helen Weigle, 77, Tippecanoe County

One thing that was nice; they never left us in the school; they shooed us out. You went outdoors and played outside, unless it was rainy or

really bad. Then we played inside, of course. We had half the school
floor space [to play in inside].
Dorothy Hoffman, 59, Adams County

Down in the basement on rainy days we played Skip To My Lou
and Drop the Handkerchief.
Sadie Davis, 78, Decatur County

And on rainy days, we'd play forfeits. Each person would give the
leader something then [he'd hold it over a person's head] and say
"Heavy, heavy hangs over thy head" and then they'd say "What shall
be done to redeem it?" Then the other person would say something like
"Recite the multiplication table" or something like that.
Grace Heinzman, 86, Hamilton County

In the wintertime [inside] we would play Hi Hi Ho, which was a
game where two people held a rope, and they would keep raising it
every time. You jumped over and everyone would try to outjump the
other one. There was about three of us who were rather tall who would
always win, because we could always jump the highest, 'cause we had
the longest legs.
Dorothy Fuhrman, 40, Martin County

At the end of the day, on the last period, we had recreation. Some of
the recreations were marches we played and you got in line and went
around the schoolhouse marching. Sometimes it was playing the game
"Teakettle." If nothing else was available, our teacher always said,
"Get out your dictionary," and a word would be announced and see
who could look up that word the quickest. You were learning speed
and also how to use the dictionary.
Ellen McAfee, 68, Marshall County

We made our own fun. I was on a baseball team at the Barger
School. Because we didn't have enough boys, the girls had to play too.
We went to other grade schools around here. The teacher would load
us up and we'd go around and play other schools. We had three girls
on our team, and about every school had a girl or so. They'd chant
"The girl's up, an easy out" and we showed them sometimes they
weren't any easier to get out than some of the boys.
Dorothy Hoffman, 59, Adams County

Did they have any kind of athletics?
Yes, they played basketball outside. Then my last year they built a

new school building and they had a gymnasium in it. So the girls got to play basketball, but we always had to wear long-sleeved white middy blouses and long bloomers that were dark blue. Didn't dare to let any skin show!

Lois Wagoner, 76, Fulton County

Recess at a one-room school.
The children are playing a circle game.
Submitted by an Extension Homemaker

I can remember the basketball girls. We had knickers to play in. Some of the more daring ones decided they were going to cut off the knickers and make like walking shorts out of them. I can remember the first night we played in them. We were wondering how the crowd was going to take them, but everything came out all right.

Ada Clarkson, 70, Jennings County

We played basketball. I played. We had a girls team then and a boys team too. We didn't come home after school and go back to practice or to a game. We couldn't afford that. One trip was all we could make. We would stay for practice or to go to the ball game.

But they was different than they are today. There wasn't any pressure on anybody. Parents wasn't interested—not many parents ever went to a ball game. We played for fun. The teacher was the coach. No one was ever on the coach that he didn't coach right. We tried to win, but it wasn't anything like it's got to be today.

Catherine Summers, 67, Harrison County

We never had a chance to play basketball and baseball like the girls do today. I wish we had, but it was all for the boys, the boys got to do everything. I won at ping pong. We had ping pong and I won ping pong awards in high school.

Sharon Windhorst, 35, Fayette County

Our fun, I guess, was basketball. Of course, this is Indiana and that's the big thing, is basketball. I was a cheerleader, but we didn't have the following for basketball games like they do now.

We usually took a bus from one school to another. The cheerleaders got to ride on the bus. When we'd go away from home, the cheer section was the second team yelling for the first team, and the first team yelling for the second team. That was our cheer section.

But at home there was quite a following; quite a few of the parents came.

About everybody in the school had to play, no more than we had in the school. All played that could, because there weren't that many students.

Dorothy Hoffman, 59, Adams County

One celebration I missed and it just hurt me. When I was in the eighth grade Franklin had a very good basketball team and Hopewell had a very good team. Franklin beat Hopewell, which was a great event. The next morning the kids from Franklin, I guess 100 at least, got a box and covered it with black and walked out to Hopewell and sang Franklin songs and walked back to Franklin. It was a five mile trip out there and five miles back.

Because of that impropriety, Franklin was not allowed to play in the tournament. They were kicked out. But Fuzzy Vandiver and John Gant, two of the Wonder Five boys, were in my class. Immediately after that they became such stars in basketball in high school, and nobody ever held that march against them.

Beulah Mardis, 76, Johnson County

SPECIAL DAYS

Do you remember any kinds of special events at the school?
Yes, Christmastime. We always put on a program for the parents. They'd come and bring a carry-in dinner and we always had a Christmas program.
   Dorothy Hoffman, 59, Adams County

   When Christmastime come along, why some of the parents would go cut a tree out of the woods and then the parents would come in whenever our Christmas dinner was going to be.
   They put boards on top of the desks, and made the tables and then they put this tree in the corner, and they spread sheets around it.
   And all the time, the teacher was going along with the school, and the parents were back there decorating the tree (laughs). It was decorated with popcorn and cranberries. It was a pretty tree, we thought it was, at least.
   So after dinner was over, they opened up the Christmas tree and we had a little program (we always had a program, pert near every holiday) and when the program was over, the presents were distributed and Santa came and gave them presents off of the tree and, oh, it was a big day for us. We enjoyed it all.
   Mable Wingate, 89, Blackford County

   Just before Christmas, Miss Baker prepared a program and decorated a tall evergreen tree on the front stage. The curtain would be closed, and we were ordered not to peek before the afternoon program.
   Then there were many oh's and ah's as the curtain was thrown aside, for there stood the most completely beautiful tree, with sacks of candy tied with ribbon—one for each child. We gave our program of songs and recitations, and then we were dismissed for Christmas vacation.
   Lucile Imes, 82, Noble County

   I was nearly always sick around Christmastime. I had tonsillitis so bad. So one Christmas we had a teacher, well, I always liked him, but he was pretty thrifty. Well, I was sick and had to stay at home that day [Christmas program] and they had company there and another girl got my candy. He had just bought enough candy for the scholars that was there. And I never did get any treat after that. Never did.
   He was a nice man, but I never cared for him afterward. He was pretty close with his money.
   Mary Shields, 96, Blackford County

For Chirstmas, we usually had a platform—I suppose you would call it a stage—at the end of the schoolhouse where the teacher sat. They took two great big evergreen trees, one on each side of that platform, and trimmed them with popcorn. We sewed the popcorn on thread, trimmed the trees, and put some candles on it. We spoke pieces and had an evening. The parents all went.

Grace Elrod, 85, Jasper County

When it came Halloween, we had a masquerade, and I remember that it was cold, and I wore overshoes. We played games and I wore all the bottoms out of my overshoes.

Flossie Foster, 95, Hendricks County

At school we always had a May Day program. In May they had a maypole and little girls of a certain grade—fourth and fifth graders were always in that—and they had crepe paper streamers on the maypole and they had a dance that they went through and around the maypole and when they were through, the paper streamers were woven or kind of braided down that pole. If they had more than one girl in the family, that garment was handed down. All the schools had a program in the spring, and the parents would watch.

Betty Alvey, 60, Howard County

What was the school term? How late in the year did you go to school?
I would say the first of May we was usually out. We'd usually start the first of September, and about the first of May we got out.

There was always one day early in spring that the termites would come out and the whole school would be swarming with termites. We'd go outside under the trees and have class the whole day.

After they swarmed, they were gone again; but you know how they are when they swarm. The whole school would be full of termites. We'd open the windows and let them fly out. Then we would have class out under the trees that day.

Martha Werner, 63, Franklin County

I remember back when we went to school, we had spelling bees and ciphering bees. Other schools would come and visit our school and we'd stand up and spell against each other and see who could hold the longest.

The ciphering bees were the same thing, only it was arithmetic. That was always a big treat to all of us. I was good in arithmetic and I generally stood the floor many a time.

Edna Vandenbark, 92, Howard County

And maybe once a year they'd have a ciphering match and a spelling bee, and that was for anybody that wanted to come. Women and girls would bring boxes, and they could auction the boxes off.

What did the boxes have in them?

They had a supper in them. They always had sandwiches and fruit, and maybe pie or cake or cookies. The highest bidder got the box, and then you got to eat with them. If the boys knew whose the box was, they'd run it up (laughs).

What did the money go for?

Some of the time they would buy library books.

Helen Shockey, 80, Grant County

Opal: About the only entertainment we had in school was pie suppers. When we got big enough to take a pie and a boy would buy it, we thought we were grown up then, just real big.

Juanita: We had to wear dresses down to our shoe tops, then.

Opal Whitsett, 84, and Juanita Hunter, 81, Scott County

Have you ever been involved in a box social?

Oh, when I went to common school, to grade school, we had one every winter. It was a lot of fun.

Tell us about it.

Well, the girls would fill a box full of food, and dress the box up in bows and ribbons and crepe paper and anything to make it pretty. Then an auctioneer would auction the boxes off. And the boyfriends and every Tom, Dick and Harry was there to bid on them.

The highest bidder got the box, and the one who bought the box got to eat the meat out of the box with the girl who brought it. That was a lot of fun and I guess it has brought lovers together in the past.

Then was the money used for some worthy cause?

Yes, maybe they'd buy some equipment for the library.

Agnes Bell, 85, Hamilton County

The last day of school, we always had special entertainment, and sometimes a pitch-in dinner, when the parents came.

Thelma Robeson, 71, Fayette County

Did you have a picnic on the last day of school?

Yes. They'd have a picnic. Parents would come in and bring the dinner, and they'd have a big surprise dinner on the teacher.

The teacher expected it every year?

Yes, the teacher expected it. And then they'd have a program after the dinner ended. That was usual.

Our grandfather had a phonograph that played cylinder records. And on the last day of school at the school where we were going, he was invited to bring the phonograph and he played those records for the last day of school program.

Lennie Hern, 90, Decatur County

Water for the school often came from the wells of people who lived close to the school. Going to fetch the water was a much-sought-after chore.
Submitted by Blackford County

I remember one time for the last day of school, we'd have a big dinner and a program. And then the teacher would call on some of the patrons maybe to get up and say a few things.

Then we always had a spelling bee for the entertainment. And I noticed that day, when we were there, some of the mothers were dressed a lot nicer than my mother was, and I just felt a little ashamed of her dress.

And you know, they had that spelling bee, and she was the last one standing up! They stood everybody who wanted to spell clear around the schoolhouse; and she was the last one standing up! So I changed my mind about my mother! I didn't see that dress then (chuckles).

Mary Wolf, 88, Huntington County

When I graduated from Shake Rag [School] I went to Wadesville to take my examination.

An examination to graduate from high school?

Yes. It was a written examination on spelling, arithmetic, reading, physiology, grammar, English, geography and history. You had to have a 75 to pass, and mine was a 90. I thought it was pretty good.

Vernell Saltzman, 81, Posey County

At that time to pass the eighth grade, you had to take a test, and the teacher I had in the seventh grade thought it would be a good idea that my girlfriend and I have a chance at taking the test a year early.

As it happened, I passed all the tests except one, and it was history. You were allowed to fail in two of them, and still go on to high school. So here I had started high school without having to go through the eighth grade.

Inez Walthers, 70, Jasper County

In those days, to graduate from the eighth grade, you had to take an examination, a day long examination.

On everything you had learned?

Yes, all the subjects. From writing to geography and mathematics—all of them.

All the eighth grade students in the county had to go to the court-house. The county superintendent conducted the examination. We had time for lunch. We wrote on those examination questions for an entire day. To go on to high school, you had to make an average of 75 percent or above on all subjects.

A lot of students didn't go to high school in those days. Not because they couldn't pass the test, but because there were no school buses and if they lived in the country they had no access to high school facilities. They couldn't get to the high school in many cases.

Blanche Burnett, 77, Morgan County

I graduated from common school and then quit. You had to walk into Nashville to continue schooling, and that was an eight to ten mile walk, one way.

Iva Kelp, 74, Brown County

I just went to the eighth grade. My folks wanted me to go to high school, but I knew more than they did, then. I thought I did. I didn't want to, and they didn't push you.

Bertha Pampel, 83, Benton County

In those days they had graduation at the end of the eighth grade; because girls weren't expected to go on to school. What was the use of going to school? They were just going to get married anyway. So we weren't encouraged to go beyond the eighth grade.

Neva Schlatter, 79, Pulaski County

Well, I graduated from common school. We had commencements in those days and we had the commencement exercise at Pleasant Hill School. We had a big time.

Each one of us had to say something on that program and I know my subject was The Value of a Reputation. I sweat blood over that.

And then, to top it all off, they built a platform out on the south side of the church, and they had the Cumback [local school] band up there to play a good while before the commencement exercises ever begun. So it was a really big event.

Pearl McCall, 89, Daviess County

Was the eighth grade a special time for you?

Yes, we had a special party with our relatives all there; aunts and uncles, cousins. The last month at the grade school, we had to go into Oldenburg for our solemn communion. We were supposed to have went the whole year, but since my mother had died and I had to do quite a bit of the work at home, I got a special dispensation, so I only had to go one month before school was out to go to Oldenburg so we could make our solemn communion. And we still had graduation from school.

Tell me about solemn communion.

The Catholic parish, they celebrate this special communion with the graduation from school.

Were there any special clothes?

Yes, we all had to wear white dresses and veils and white shoes and we all carried a lighted candle and went into church, then we put it on the altar, which was a very significant thing.

There were pictures taken after the Mass, and then we went home and celebrated all day.

Martha Werner, 63, Franklin County

GROWING UP
HEALTHY

*"My grandmother had no use for a doctor.
She had had fourteen children,
and she figured she knew more than the doctor did anyway.*

*You had to be real desperately sick.
If an onion poultice wasn't going to do any good,
or a mustard poultice, or a good physic,
then you began to think about a doctor."*

Neva Schlatter, 79, Pulaski County

The doctor came in his horse and buggy
to the patient's bedside when called.
His small bag held his entire
range of medicines.
Submitted by Rush County

BIRTH

Would you tell us where you were born?
I was born at home on the farm. I had a midwife; Mrs. Sarah Werner was the midwife who delivered me 96 years ago.
Pearl Hiland, 96, Fulton CountyCounty

I was born without a doctor in attendance. In fact, my mother was all alone at the time. She had sent my five-year-old brother after a neighbor lady, but she didn't get there in time. But that was not an uncommon occurrence in those days. We were four miles from a doctor. We had no telephone. The only way to get a doctor was to go after one in a horse and buggy—rather a slow process, especially for such an occasion.
Ruth Snyder, 83, Marshall County

Your mother's children were all born at home?
All born at home. But there's somebody always went and got the doctor. There was always a doctor there, except me. Grandma delivered me.
Edna Winter, 74, Pulaski County

Suppose there was a child born in the family, what happened then?
The doctor would come to the home and a neighbor would come in and help take care of the baby. They washed it and cleaned it up and then the doctor would come back—I guess it was the third day—he would come back to see the mother. She would have to stay in bed for nine days. On the 10th day she would get up. She wore a band around her stomach.
The neighbors would come in and look after the baby. I forget how the housework got done, whether my father did it, or some of the older children.
Did they put a band around the baby's abdomen, too?
Yes, they used to call them belly bands. And at that time the babies wore big, long dresses.
How long did they nurse a baby usually?
For a year or fifteen months.
Francis Harley, 89, Marshall County

I remember when my youngest sister was born. At that time when children were born at home, everyone would come in. All of us kids were chased outside to play. I don't know if we really realized what was happening, but then later there was this little baby. Nothing was said. I don't even remember mother looking pregnant.

Were you told ahead of time that a new baby was coming?

I don't think so.

Juanita Harden, 49, Bartholomew County

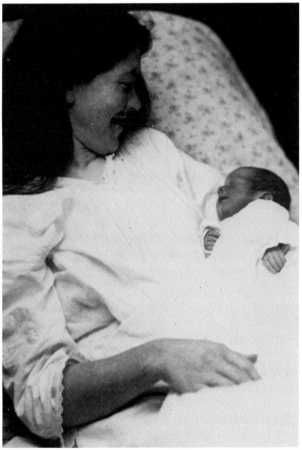

A mother relaxes with her baby in her
arms after a home birth.
Submitted by Whitley County

In those days the doctor came to the home to deliver babies. Young girls, maybe 17 or 18 years old, came in and helped take care of the baby. I was named for the two that came in and helped take care of me when I was a baby. I was named for Gertrude Esther Garst and Gladys Beulah Mallot. My name is Beulah Esther. Those girls took every other day, coming in and caring for me when I came into this world.

Beulah Grinstead, 68, Hamilton County

And you were born here in St. Phillips?

Right. All of my sisters and brothers were born in St. Phillips in the home.

Did your mother have someone to care for her?

Oh yes, there was a Mrs. Rheinhardt that came in. She was always there when the children were born. She was a widow lady, and that was what she did.

Do you have any idea of what her responsibilities were?

I don't know what she did when the birth was going on, but I know she came out for hot water and things like that. Then she would come every morning after the child was born to bath the baby. At that time the mother stayed in bed for ten days, or maybe two weeks.

And she would take care of the baby while the mother was still in bed?

Right, and then there would be some women came in sometimes and prepared the meals, because some of us were born in the summertime while there was harvest going on, and Mom had to have a cook for the men.

Of course, when my youngest brother was born, us girls were there and we did the cooking and washing.

Thelma Roehr, 69, Posey County

But the folks in our time, always seemed like little babies died. They lost so many babies.

Alvah Watson, 97, Allen County

How many were in your family? Was it eight?

Ten. Of course, the first three babies didn't live. My mother's first babies were triplets—three boys. Of course, back then they didn't have incubators. One lived a short while, one a day or two and one lived about a week. They all died.

Vida Mundy, 89, Lawrence County

I was born on May 6, and they say it was 11:00 in the morning. I've heard the story so many times I feel like I was there. Actually, I was, but I just can't verify it for the truth. They said I weighed two pounds. Mother's sister was there, and she took and put me in Mother's butter bowl and kicked the fire out of the kitchen stove and put me in the oven. I laid there for six days, and you know you can make zwieback in four days. I was really baked dry. People called me their oven-baked baby. But after 97 years I now weigh 122½ pounds. As you can see, I held my own and gained a little.

Alvah Watson, 97, Allen County

DISEASES

I think back, we did have more diseases, because we didn't have the medicines and vaccines that we have today.

Ellen Doss, 34, Clark County

TB was very common when I can first remember, and it'd go clear through a family. If one person in the family died from TB, it was almost sure to be several in that same family before long would have it. And they didn't have any cure for that, either.

The very first they did anything for it, that I can remember about, was completely isolate the person. They usually built a little house out in the yard someplace, so they just had to live in that, alone, to keep the rest of the family from getting the disease.

It isn't considered a fatal disease now at all.

Virgie Bowers, 81, Pulaski County

I think TB was dreaded the most. Some called it consumption, and they called it congested lungs.

Ruth Dye, 75, Martin County

My sister had tuberculosis and I was ten when she died. And I really missed her. She was ten years older than me, but she was more like a mother to me than she was like a sister. She took care of me so much. We were really close.

Ozetta Sullivan, 72, Harrison County

My mother, when I was three, contracted tuberculosis and spent two years in the Smith-Esteb Tuberculin Sanatorium. My father worked for the railroad in Greencastle, so that necessitated my living with aunts and uncles. No one wanted a little kid for the entire duration, so I lived in seven different homes over a two year period.

Deanna Barricklow, 41, Fayette County

I remember, as a small child, there was someone who had consumption. Of course that was tuberculosis. And no one wanted to get anywhere near them because it was catching.

The same way with cancer. They didn't want to use anything that had been used by a cancer patient. Everything that had been theirs was supposed to be burned after they were gone.

Neva Schlatter, 79, Pulaski County

Prevention and treatment of tuberculosis
was the subject of wide
public education publicity.
American Lung Association Collection
Indiana Historical Society

My half-sister was eighteen months old when she died. And they decided that the only way to raise me was to move out of that house. That was what people used to do. If there was tuberculosis in a house, they moved out. They had no way of knowing how to overcome it.

So we bought this home, and moved here. Tuberculosis had been prevalent in the old house. An older aunt had died with it and my grandmother had it, and then my sister contracted it.

[Later] I had pneumonia, and my mother said they never changed my clothes for three months all over. They would scoot up a little and wash that part of me, and then cover [that] up and wash another part, but they never [un]dressed me for three months.

Was that because of the pneumonia?

Yes, and, of course, I was a candidate for tuberculosis.

Beulah Mardis, 76, Johnson County

My mother died from TB and she was hospitalized for fourteen months before. This does leave quite a lasting impression on you, when you are fourteen years old, when you lose a parent. That was always one of the big fears of my life.

I understand you did have tuberculosis between your third and fourth child?

Right. And I was only hospitalized eight and a half weeks. I found that they had new medications and I found that the hospitalization was much shorter, and you were not always going to die from it. So now that takes away all of the fear.

Delores Slater, 52, Porter County

There was 20 of the kids at school got typhoid fever. And I got it, and I was so sick with that stuff. The doctor came out. I was in bed with it for nine weeks. I just thought I would never get over it.

Those days they starved you about, because it was just liquids and a little light stuff. Nowadays they feed you real good to get you over it better.

Anyhow, I couldn't even walk, I was so sick. All my hair came out and I was so poor and skinny. That was in November, and I didn't get to go to school the rest of the year. I was 11 years old and I had to learn to walk all over.

There was a lot of the children that died with it.

Masa Scheerer, 82, Huntington County

When I was a child, my family had typhoid fever. I didn't have it, but four of the children did. A well was contaminated, and we had to quit using water out of that well.

How did the doctor treat you for that?

I think they starved them, almost. They didn't know what to do then, like they do now. My brother older than I nearly died with it. I had a little brother took it and they gave him baths in lukewarm water. His stomach would swell, and I think that's what they did it for.

They would put beef in a can, cut up fresh beef with no water on it and boil it, like we cold pack meat now. They put a lid on and boiled it until the juice came out of that beef. And they would feed that, a few drops or teaspoons full at a time to give him a little bit of nourishment. It was called beef tea. It was pure juice out of the meat, no water.

Did you get fresh water you could trust from somewhere else?

There was another well on the place, and they tested it. I remember the doctor taking great large bottles and sending them away for analysis. They tested the other well and it was all right.

And my oldest brother was so sick, and he nearly died of it. And I remember the neighbors, it was fall and time to make apple butter. In those days everybody made apple butter outside in a kettle. We had a big orchard, and everybody came in. And because he was so ill, they whispered. They didn't make any noise and they made apple butter out on the lawn, at night.

Agnes Bell, 85, Hamilton County

I had diphtheria back in 1919. Mother thought I had tonsillitis and she was trying to doctor, and they [finally] got the doctor out. There was three of us had it in the neighborhood. The two boys didn't make it, but I made it.

But I was a mighty sick girl for a while. The aftereffects of diphtheria is worse than the disease, really.

Did it leave you with some kind of ailment?

Yes, my throat was kind of paralyzed. I would drink and it would come out of my nose. Then my eyes—they weren't crossed, but one went out and one went in. It set me back for quite a while, and that is a terrible disease, because most of the people didn't make it.

Bertha Pampel, 83, Benton County

We had a younger brother and a younger sister [who] had polio back before polio was very common. Our family doctor brought other doctors once in a while when he was making his calls, just for them to see a case.

They'd get a mixture of ether and alcohol at the drugstore that they used for a sort of massage. I think we bought gallons of that that my mother used on my brother. She would use it two or three times a day, rubbing it in.

He came through it a lot better than some children did. But he's been a little bit handicapped, too, all of his life.

The thing they used for the rest of us children, to prevent us from taking polio, was to gargle peroxide in our throat several times during the day.

Beulah Rawlings, 76, Hamilton County

Lois, my sister, had infantile paralysis, and it left her badly crippled. She was five years old. My mother told the doctor from the start that she was so afraid that Lois had infantile paralysis, because there had been some cases around. He said he knew it was just worms, and he doctored her for worms.

My sister took care of her when there wasn't any school, because my mother had so much to do. She said, "Mom, did you know that Lois can't walk," and Mom said, "No!" And she said, "Well, I'm going to put her down and you have her come over to you." And when Lois started over, she fell. And from that time on, her head drew 'way back and her eyes rolled back in her head. We had the doctor out again, but he would not have it, that it was infantile paralysis.

It was maybe not quite a year after Lois had this that Wilma was born. And the doctor came, of course, to deliver the baby. Mom said, "Now I want you to look at Lois walk, and I believe you'll have to say that she has had infantile paralysis." So they brought Lois in, and she walked over on the side of her foot and threw that leg and her body twisted and he said, "Yes, Candace, I'll have to say you were right." But how she ever came through that, with him doctoring her for worms, I don't know.

Mary Sheeks, 73, Lawrence County

My sister Irene, she had some kind of rheumatism [and she] was bedfast nearly that whole summer. And it left her with crooked knees and when she learned to walk after she got better, she'd pull her stockings up real tight across her knees and then she could walk.

Mary Wolf, 88, Huntington County

When I was twelve I had rheumatic fever. One Monday I couldn't walk any more, so they called the doctor. That's when they would come to your house. He told me to go right to bed and stay there. I was in bed for six months, from January to June.

The doctor told me never to raise my hands over my head. We had brass beds then, and I was pulling myself up one time, and he said never to do anything like that again.

The only medicine I can remember taking when I had rheumatic fever was a powder that was folded up in a little piece of paper. It would be put in a teaspoon and I would take it. Now that I have tasted aspirin, I'm sure all it was was aspirin that I was taking for my rheumatic fever.

Florence DeYoung, 68, Jasper County

When Joe [husband] was seven, fourteen, and twenty-eight he had rheumatiz and just crippled up and just couldn't go. After his heart started bothering him, he went to [the doctors] and they asked him, "Have you ever had rheumatic fever?" and Joe said, "Well, back then they called it just rheumatiz," and they told him "Well, you have scars on your heart and they didn't form overnight." So evidently it was rheumatic fever, but back then they didn't know—just called it rheumatiz.

Vida Mundy, 89, Lawrence County

Smallpox was quite a threat. The immunization later took care of it, but when it first came around, it was quite a threat.

Eula Kelso, 78, Lawrence County

In Mansfield, they had a case of smallpox. People were so afraid of it. They would go around and walk down the railroad.

Clyde Smith, 92, Parke County

We had a round of smallpox once. My younger brother was sick, just really pretty sick. The doctor had been there two or three times. He came one night and he had been to see another boy in the community and the two cases were pretty much alike. My mother said, "If he'd broken out you'd think he had smallpox." But he said, "Oh, he didn't have smallpox." But during the night he got to feeling better and went to sleep. Mother turned up the kerosene light and saw some bumps coming out. The next morning she called the doctor and told him he [son] had smallpox.

We all had vaccinations.

So smallpox went through the whole community?

Oh, yes. School had to close up a little bit for it.

People died of it, I suppose.

Oh, yes.

Beulah Rawlings, 76, Hamilton County

When smallpox returned to the neighborhood, they [grandparents and family] survived the smallpox. Emily took the children outside the home and lined them up. She took a sewing needle and scratched the upper left arm until it bled. The she went into the house and took some of the pus from the pox and put it in the blood and vaccinated her children. My father had a larger scar than I did from the smallpox vaccination.

Essie Rumble, 77, Gibson County

When you were young, did you have any illnesses?
I had chicken pox, and whooping cough, and measles five times.
Measles five times?
The last time was when I was 30 years old. Everytime I was exposed, I would get them. I didn't build up an immunity.
  Blanche Martin, 77, Tippecanoe County

I had the whooping cough, and the doctor didn't know what was the matter until I whooped. I took a cold and my father said, "You take this little bottle and go to the drug store and tell them you want something to stop your cold." Well, it stopped some and I went to school for a week while I took that medicine, and then the doctor said, "You had better not send her to school." I never got to go any more. They had to hold me in bed when I started to whoop, and I couldn't eat anything.
I was in fractions, in the fifth grade, and they were hard for me after that, but I finally learned them. But I remember when I had the whooping cough.
  Flossie Foster, 95, Hendricks County

I was a sickly child. I had a lot of pneumonia as a child. My mother gave birth to me in my aunt's house. And her [aunt's] child came home that day with whooping cough. So at the age of three weeks I caught whooping cough and nearly died. I had to sleep on my mother's chest for about three months, because I constantly coughed. And I was the sickliest child because of the pneumonia and the bronchial problems from having whooping cough as a baby.
  Sue Cole, 43, Harrison County

My one brother had whooping cough real bad, and it left him affected. He was just never real well after having whooping cough.
How old was he?
He was forty. He was married and had three children.
  Eula Kelso, 78, Lawrence County

What was so bad about whooping cough?
Oh, they could choke to death. They couldn't catch their breath. They would whoop! And this phlegm would come and they couldn't get it out. It was serious.
I had one brother that had lots of croup. A croup cough sounds a lot like whooping cough, only they don't vomit with it. They just can't get their breath, and they turn blue. My dad would run his finger down that kid's throat and pull out this long rope of phlegm and he would

get his breath and away we'd go again.
  Edna Winter, 74, Pulaski County

My sister, I can't remember whether she had measles and took whooping cough, had whooping cough and took measles, but she got pneumonia and she died. She was only a little over a year old.
  They didn't have all this medicine they have now.
  Helen Shockey, 80, Grant County

How did it happen that your dad had never had the measles?
  Because you run from those things. There wasn't a lot of contact with people. If something [disease] was in the neighborhood, you stayed home.
  But with consolidated schools and the kind of transportation [we have now] it just don't take anything like that but a few days until it's everywhere. But back in those days, maybe only one or two families in the whole community would get it, because you just weren't in close contact all the time.
  Edna Winter, 74, Pulaski County

When I was about thirteen, my father had never had measles, and he took them at that time, and then took pneumonia. The doctor went home and told his wife he'd have to make out a death certificate the next morning. He pulled through and lived to be eighty years old.
  Thelma Robeson, 72, Fayette County

One winter, one of the boys came to school with measles. So about a week later, school was closed because everybody had the measles, being it was a one-room school and everybody [was] exposed at the same time.
  Maurice [brother] and I were kept in the same room. He was sick and I wasn't. I insisted on light and would get up and put up the window blinds when Mother was out of the room. Both of us have worn glasses ever since.
  Harriett Gwinnup, 73, Fayette County

Before I was born, my sister had scarlet fever. My father had decided that one child was enough [if they were going] to be able to give her what they would like, because he had come from a family of fourteen children and it had been rather rough going for him.
  But after my sister had scarlet fever and they almost lost her, then Mother decided they should have another child. So that's how I happened to come along.
  Ada Clarkson, 70, Jennings County

When I was five years old I had scarlet fever. The doctor came to the house at that time, and we were quarantined. My sisters couldn't go to school and they sealed up a back room on our house so that Dad could stay in there.They moved a bed in for him. He would get out groceries and set them on the porch. We had a coal stove and he would carry the coal around every night and morning.

The doctor would come to the house and call every week to see how we were doing. After about three weeks of that, my younger brother who was only three took the fever from me. They had to give him shots of what they called antitoxin because it had settled in his chin and he had a big abscess on his chin. It drained him so he had to learn to walk all over again, because he had lost so much weight and was so little and thin.

We spent Christmas in quarantine. The first week we were out, the health officer came around to the house and they fumigated the house and sprayed everyone as you went out the door. We had to go stay with Grandma overnight, because they would burn candles in your house for so many hours before you could come back. It was supposed to kill all the germs.

Betty Alvey, 60, Howard County

Did they quarantine? Did they actually put a sign on the door?

Oh, yes. A red tag.

What did it say? What did it look like?

Well, the diphtheria ones, they were great big red tags and they were tacked on the side of the house facing the road. And they said DIPH-THERIA in big black letters on this sign. And scarlet fever was the same way.

Edna Winter, 74, Pulaski County

One time I had scarlet fever and it formed an abscess on my neck and that was terrible. I remember my mother had taken us to the doctor and in the meantime they came down and quarantined us in. My father was a railroad worker and he came and they wouldn't let him in the house. So he stayed with cousins. Every morning before he'd go to work he'd get up and he'd come over and he'd look in the window at us. And every evening, as soon as he got off work, he'd come back to the window and we'd talk to him through the window.

And I often think of my mother, taking care of us children, there in the house all alone.

Hazel Norden, 76, DeKalb County

**I was thinking about pneumonia [which was] an illness they didn't
have the drugs to fight that they do now. So many children had pneumonia in the winter, and a fever they just couldn't control.**

Pneumonia was almost a fatal disease then, because they didn't have
any medical remedies that would really work. They had some ideas
that worked on home remedies, but it wasn't a cure for it like they
have now.

Virgie Bowers, 81, Pulaski County

Homegrown dentistry.
J. C. Allen Collection

My mother could always take care of us and doctor us. Very few
times can I remember having the doctor at our house. She would call
on the telephone and he would tell her what to do. I remember one

time that I had a nephew that was very ill. He had double pneumonia. The doctor came several times and he said he had done all he could.

My mother said she had a few cures herself, and he said, "If you would know what to do, you go ahead and do it." She made plasters out of milk and bread and mustard and she put them on him all night. The next morning the doctor came back and he was definitely better. He said, "Your cure helped, all right, and I thought he wouldn't have lived through the night." So she doctored us all.

Elma Matthew, 74, Madison County

My oldest sister had pneumonia, and she was doctored with fried onion poultices so much that my mother could never stand to eat cooked onions after that.

Then a few years after that, another sister had pneumonia and the doctor came one morning and said she wouldn't live through the day. He didn't do anything for her comfort. My grandmother, on that round, made pumpkin seed poultices and worked with her and pulled her through.

Beulah Rawlings, 76, Hamilton County

My grandfather, I remember well, he had double pneumonia and the doctor had prescribed analgesic balm. It came in a tin can and it was just like putty, and it was supposed to be smeared on him.

Well, after the doctor left, instead of putting that on him my grandma went downstairs and fried onions and when they were real hot she put them in a cloth and put them on Grandpa. As soon as that cooled a little, she would have another one ready to put on.

One time the doctor came back unexpectedly and opened the door and smelled the onions. He said, "I know what you've done!" and he scolded her and had her take them [onions] off and put this analgesic balm on him.

Did he get better after that?

Yes, he got better.

Evelyn Buchanan, 78, Scott County

In the days before every sizable community had a hospital, serious illness was an entirely different situation. At times like that, neighbors and families supported one another, in ways that have gone with modern medical facilities and easier quicker transportation.

The winter after Paul's [brother] first birthday, he suddenly became seriously ill with pneumonia. Our family doctor had come and gone, saying there was nothing more he could do. Dorothy [sister] and I stayed home from school to take over the housework, while Mother and Father cared for Paul.

The second morning, as the younger children got on the school bus, our Aunt Kate Stephenson Scott climbed off the bus with her suitcase in her hand. All she knew was that her son had come home from school saying that someone must be sick at Claude's house, because he and two of the girls had missed school.

She announced herself ready to stay for as long as she was needed, and that's just what she did. She sent Dorothy and I back to school; took over managing the house and helped with Paul, too.

Later that day our uncle Kermit Tower, a resident doctor at Long Hospital in Indianapolis, also came to stay and care for the baby. Kermit started some different treatment for Paul which included hot packs on his chest around the clock for days. Kermit performed one surgery in our house and another one in Dr. Deen's office.

It was a long, slow process, involving all the family, but with everyone working together, Paul was on his way to recovery by spring.

Helen Ridge, Crawford County

ACCIDENTS

There was an old Auntie that always lived at the farm. It was my father's mother's sister, and she had been hurt when she was a child. Her father was splitting wood and she got hit in the head with an ax, and it made a dent in her skull. In those days, they knew nothing to do. She laid unconscious for days, and she grew up with a mind that wasn't the way it should be.

Margaret Butler, Steuben County

I remember a time when my brother was run over with the manure spreader. The wheel went across his head and this bone [indicating forehead] was pushed down over his eye. He didn't have any eye. They were going to take him to the doctor in Fort Wayne for an operation.

It was May day, and some neighbor kids had come in to see him, and they were romping around, and he was romping around, too, and this bone popped back into place. So they never had to have an operation.

Bernice Esch, 70, Lagrange County

One hot summer hay-making day [Grandfather] had a severe headache and had to lie down. J. Harold Tower, about 18, was delegated to be foreman of the hay-making crew.

The two day laborers were not too proficient regarding unloading hay. J. Harold had set the fork in the loose hay and was to jump off the wagon before the fork was tripped. Communication was poor, and the massive fork laden with hay was tripped before it reached the [haymow]. It came down full force on J. Harold and slashed his skull.

He was taken to the front yard and first aid [was being] administered, when along this country road came one of the very few cars seen in those days.

The sight-seeing occupants were a surgeon and his nurse wife. They stopped and applied their many skills and [saved] Harold's life. He carried a horrendous skull scar the remainder of his life.

Help came from the right place at the right time.

Ethel Tower, Crawford County

DEATH

I am the oldest child. I have a sister five years younger. A little baby was born when I was 10, during the influenza epidemic in 1918. Our mother almost didn't live, and the baby didn't live.

I remember coming home. I knew there was a baby because I had looked in the dresser drawers and saw the pretty outing flannel things with crocheted edges, and I knew there was [going to be] a baby, but they didn't tell the children then.

When I came home one evening, there was my father with this tiny, tiny baby trying to feed it with a medicine dropper, and Dad wouldn't let me see my mother.

Grandmother told me to do my chores. I had rabbits to feed and chickens to tend.

When I came in, the baby wasn't in the room. I looked in the front room and the little baby was on a blanket on the piano bench. I started to weep and Grandmother said, "Don't you let out one tiny yelp. Your mother is so sick. You'll make her more sick than she is." So I high-tailed it out of there.

Ilo Coffing, 76, Montgomery County

I remember one night in 1894 and my mother said to me, "Would you mind going over to my sister, Aunt Rena?" (that was her sister that lived across the highway). "Go over and ask if she'd come over, Baby's awful sick." And I said, "Oh, sure."

I was brave, I was only about nine years old, but between our house and her house there was a bridge to cross the creek. I went out and the moon was shining bright, which was a help. I just went down the road as far as I could go. And when I come to that bridge, I stopped. I was afraid to cross the bridge. So finally I just backed up and made one leap and I went over the bridge.

I remember knocking at the door and my aunt said, "Who is it?" And I told her Mommy wanted to know if she'd come over, that baby Grafton is awful sick. And she said, "Yes, you wait until I dress."

I waited for her and when we went back to the bridge, no trouble at all.

But when we got home, my brother had died.

Oh, it seemed nearly every neighborhood had a baby that died when they were quite young. And our house was no exception.

The neighbors were going to go together and take their dinners and have a surprise for an uncle in the family. When they drove in, the man they were going to have the dinner for was out in the barn cutting boards. He was making a coffin, a rough box for a baby that had died the day before. We didn't know about it till we got there, because there was no telephones. And we were having a picnic dinner for him, and found him making a box for their baby that had died. So there was lots of sadness.

Alvah Watson, 97, Allen County

My oldest brother had cancer and died, at the age of 20. And Mother held up under that. I think back now, and it's unbelievable how she held up.

He was there one winter and was very, very sick. His wife and little girl, was there, too. They had had to move back and she [mother] had to keep the rest of us quiet and busy, because he was bedfast. Then, after he died, his wife and little girl went back to live with her folks. And I remember this neighbor lady saying, "I don't see how you can be so happy when you've just lost a son, or be the way you are." I remember my mother's answer was, "I've got seven other children to make life happy for, and, although I think about his death, I can't dwell on it."

Mildred Weaver, 64, Pulaski County

DOCTORS
AND NURSES

We stayed at home and our mother and daddy doctored us. We didn't have any hospital, and the doctor was over at Scottsburg and that was five miles away. We didn't have any telephone, either, at that time, so we seldom called a doctor.

Sometimes, when people had serious things wrong with them, the

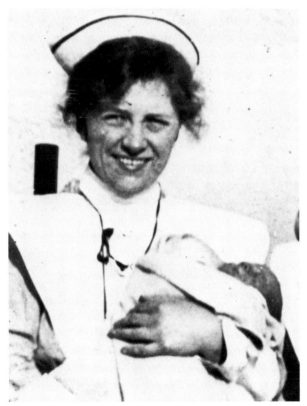

Both professional and home nursing care were very important. This professional nurse was employed at the Methodist Hospital in Indianapolis.
Submitted by Rush County

doctor would be called, and he would drive his horse and buggy and come. They made house calls at that time.

But neighbors would be very good to help in case of sickness in the family. If there was a bad sickness and they needed someone to help out, someone always stayed all night.

Zelma Blocher, 81, Scott County

Yes, the doctors made home visits, but the doctors were often scarce and you just couldn't get one. They came in their horse and buggy and if another patient was sick, well, you just waited till the doctor got through with him and got on to your house.

Margaret Larson, Porter County

We had the last telephone on the road here. A doctor in Alexandria would take his little Ford and go out through here. His wife would call and leave messages here for him, so he would know where to go next. Every day she would call out and he would come in, or call, to find out where he was to go next.

Sometimes he would stop in and get in behind the stove and rest a while and warm up.

Elma Matthew, 74, Madison County

Doctor Roberts was over at West Point, Kentucky. He would come across the Ohio River and doctor you. One of the things I remember was when we was in grade school. I can't remember why, we all had to be vaccinated. I think there was an epidemic of smallpox. So Dr. Roberts just came over to Lon Miller's house and we all met him there. And he vaccinated all of us at one time.

Catherine Summers, 67, Harrison County

The doctor came to the house, but I know my father would say, "Now we won't call the doctor before 7:00 in the morning or after 9:00 in the evening." And he held to that very strictly.

Because he respected the doctor's time.

Dora Giggy, 79, Lagrange County

We were never sick very much, but when we were Dr. Ward came from Georgetown to see us. He left very bad tasting medicine. If we had toothaches, he pulled our teeth. He was with Mother when two or three of we children were born. If we didn't have money to pay him, he was given a stack of hay or some bushels of corn for his horse.

Violet David, 79, Brown County

I hated to take medicine. They had to hold me down and pour it down my throat. All medicine was liquid then. I can still see myself on that couch. I remember it was liquid and brown.
Margaret Gibson, 87, Cass County

There used to be a druggist in Bridgeton and he was pretty good. He was about like a doctor. They would go to him first, see what he could do. If they possibly had to, then they'd go to a doctor.
Stella Irwin, 84, Parke County

I think that many of the things that we go to the doctor for are things we'd get over anyway, if we didn't go (laughs). Maybe I've inherited some of my grandmother's ideas about doctors.
Neva Schlatter, 79, Pulaski County

You just think back 50 years, how many new and wonderful things have come, just in your lifetime.
We used to have our teeth pulled, you know. They never froze it or anything. You had to go, and they'd just pull them out.
Bessie Werner, 80, Pulaski County

We would only go to the dentist if we had a very severe toothache.
Martha Werner, 63, Franklin County

Mother had trouble with her teeth. Father took us to town and he went on to do something else. But I was supposed to stay with Mother.
We went to the dentist. He had two little rooms, and he had a stove that had warm water on.
My mother went in there and she had 26 teeth taken out. He told her to lay in there [other room] and I was to give her salt water to rinse her mouth every little while. And I remember so well, he worked on her [false] teeth and at three o'clock in the afternoon, he gave her the teeth and told her if they bothered her any to come back. Mother never went back, and she was buried with them. And those teeth were all made and she wore them home the same day, after 26 teeth had been extracted. He put them in there. That was something, wasn't it?
They wouldn't think of doing that today.
I'll never forget—the warm water, the bleeding—awful! And it wasn't very sanitary, either.
Alvah Watson, 97, Allen County

My oldest sister was about eleven years old, and she got pneumonia, and she was down. 'Course then, the doctor just came out to the house. We had no hospitals. She was so bad for about four weeks. The neighbors all came in—they came and set up at nights to help Mom, Dad and the rest to try to take care of her.

Then she started getting better and my older brother, he was 17, he took pneumonia. The doctor come out and he says to Mom and Dad, "You just can't take care of him." 'Cause they was worn out taking care of my sister. And he say, "I'll get a nurse."

So on Sunday, he come out with a nurse. She was a big red-haired woman, and she was from Canada. And we paid her $25 a week. It was awfully steep for then.

What did she do?

She took care of my brother. He was awfully sick. He was delirious for five days. She had to keep him in bed, and everything. And she fed him and looked after him. She had him up in two weeks, and it took four weeks for my sister.

Cora Keplinger, 80, Huntington County

Did you help your neighbors in time of need?

Yes, when I was growing up I always liked to go and help. I was raised that way. If there was anything you could do to help, go and do it. If you couldn't be of any help, don't be a bother. There was a nurse that gave us a few nursing lessons and I took them and they helped me an awful lot, but I always liked to help.

Anna Workman, 86, Greene County

I remember we had a neighbor and she was a "doctor." She came by our school when school started and got permission from the teacher and pupils and parents to take three hairs out of each child's head. And she'd take them down to her house. In front of the house she had a big elm tree. She would notch that [tree] and dry that hair in the tree. And she said if that healed, you would have no trouble during the winter. But if it got to running, you'd better go and see a doctor and get some medicine, because you were going to have a bad winter.

Was that very accurate?

I don't know. I never knew. But Mother always said, "Let her have three hairs. It won't hurt." But she didn't have no faith in her.

Alvah Watson, 97, Allen County

One thing I remember about my grandmother, she just made everything—medicine, salves. She was busy all the time.

Did she use the medicines and salves to doctor your family or did she

doctor for people in the neighborhood. How did she use this?
It was free to anyone who wanted to use it or anyone she thought needed it.
Did the people come to her, or did she go to them?
They came to her. Grandma seldom left the house or left her property.
Did this medicine seem to be pretty effective for people, do you remember?
Yes, it did, and I often wish that I had some of the formulas.
  Gladys Tribolet, 70, Huntington County

My mother had a lot of sick headaches and she was awfully sick and she had taken enough aspirin to get to sleep. She would always smell the camphor bottle when she got her headaches, and I felt so sorry when she was having so much trouble, so I took the camphor and poured it on her nose, while she was sleeping. Camphor is just about as hot as fire when it gets on a raw place on your skin.
Did she appreciate your help?
No, I wasn't appreciated for my kind notion. And I was being so good and helpful. I can remember I was little I had to climb up on the fainting couch to get to her, so I could get the camphor bottle to her nose.
You had to work hard to be such a help, didn't you.
Florence Nightingale, in person.
  Beulah Mardis, 76, Johnson County

It seemed like the neighbors depended on my mother when they had a family crisis or sickness in the family. She was considered a level-headed person, and they would call and ask her to come if their child had a lot of fever or had gotten hurt. They wanted her encouragement, as much as anything, I believe, and her thoughts as to whether they should call the doctor.
My mother just had a tenth grade education, but she had gotten a lot of education through the school of hard knocks. She never feared going into a home where they even had a communicable disease. I can remember her coming home and coming in the back door and stripping and saying "Throw me some clean clothes." And I don't think she ever drug anything home to the rest of the family. But she certainly went a lot of places where they had sick people.
At that time people didn't go to the hospital and a lot of deaths occurred in the home. She would be called to sit with the sick the last few hours [of their lives].
I remember one time stopping at a neighbor's, taking something she

had called and wanted me to bring. And when I got there, she was sitting beside the bed a-holding the lady's hand and sort of talking to her, telling her not to be afraid. It's pathetic when I think about it now, but this is just the type of person she was.

I suppose if she had been born 50 years [later] she would have been a nurse. But that wasn't necessary during her time. What they needed, more than anything, was just her encouragement and soothing words.

Mildred Weaver, 64, Pulaski County

HOSPITALS

No one went to the hospital then. They used to say if you went to the hospital, you went just to die. You never got well.

Gleda Stevens, Union County

When I was nine years old, my father became very ill, and the neighbors came with the horse and carriage and took him to town and then on the train to Lutheran Hospital in Fort Wayne. We had never heard of a hospital, much less of an operation. He had a gall stone and appendicitis operation. That was something very different for us, but he recovered satisfactorily.

Margaret Garrison, 82, Wabash County

My father suffered a long, long time before he would even have the surgery, because he dreaded to go into the hospital. It's a wonder he didn't have a busted appendix, but he didn't.

Eleanor Cheek, 61, Union County

I had a brother, when he was sixteen years old he had appendicitis. You know, the doctor had them to put hot hop poultices on him. They didn't advise surgery until the last resort. Had a dray wagon, an old horse thing, and had a cot in the back of it, came over here and loaded him into it and took him to the train at Worthington. They sent him to the Methodist Hospital in Indianapolis and had surgery.

My father went along. He had the surgery the same day they took him up there. My father came home and said Willie just stuck out his hand and said "Goodbye, Poppy," and he died that night.

Had they waited too long to operate?

Well, today they would say they did. Now at the first sign, they say get it out of there.

Anna Workman, 86, Greene County

I remember when I was in the third or fourth grade, I had appendicitis. I was so backward and timid. I went to school not feeling well. I spent the whole day with my head down on the desk. The teacher kept

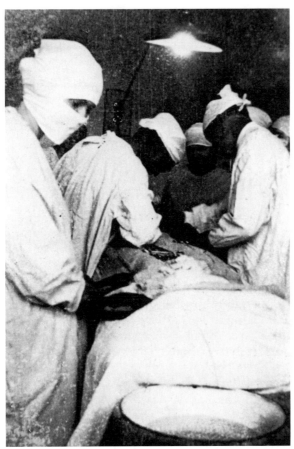

An operation in progress at the
Methodist Hospital in Indianapolis
in the 1910s.
Submitted by Rush County

asking was anything wrong, but I wouldn't say anything. I went home that evening and Mother took me to the doctor. I had surgery the next day.

Juanita Harden, 49, Bartholomew County

You had to grow flax like you grow other things in your garden. You'd let the flax [seeds] dry and if you would get a real bad pain in

your stomach or your side, or wherever, you would take these flax
seeds and put them in a bag and drop them in real hot water and wring
them out as hot as you could stand it on your hands. You would put
that on that pain.

My mother did that one night for my cousin all night long, and the
doctor told her that those flax scattered the appendicitis, but if you tell
people that nowadays, they probably wouldn't believe that.

Gaby Moon, 69, Clay County

HOME
REMEDIES

CUTS & SPRAINS

I was delivering milk down the street, and I saw someone coming to
our door. Mom wasn't home, so I started to run and I tripped over a
board and fell on a rusty nail. I was dumb in those days and I thought,
"Gee, that's nice. It didn't bleed."

In those days they didn't have the medicine they have now. Antitoxin was just starting to come in and the druggist had to go to Fort
Wayne to get tetanus antitoxin. And I was right at death's door. I was
in bed from January until almost April.

I didn't realize how bad I was. The neighbor lady came in, and
thought she'd see crepe on the door that morning, because the doctor
had said I'd either be dead in the morning, or I'd make a turn for the
better.

But it was a long time before I could walk right. It bothered my legs,
and I could walk a few steps and I'd have to set down.

Anna Surfus, 85, DeKalb County

When I was probably five or six, I was there with my grandmother—everyone else was gone—and I stepped on a rusty nail on a
board. The whole thing was in my shoe. So I yelled and here came my
grandmother. She said, "What am I going to do?" She said, "I know
what I'll do, I'll use turpentine."

First of all, she pulled out the nail, board and all, and I screamed. Then she ripped off my shoe and stuck my foot in turpentine and, today, I can still remember how badly it hurt.

But it did not get infected. It certainly didn't. It burned so badly that no germs could get in. I'll never forget that. That was probably the most traumatic thing that ever happened in my life, as far as pain is concerned.

Barbara Elliott, 54, Wells County

When I was just about seven years old, I fell down on a pitchfork. The prong went in my knee. Mommy didn't ever take us to the doctor. She just put some liniment on it and wrapped my leg up, and I had to sit in my little kid's rocking chair. I had to keep my knee out and straight until that healed up. They never hardly ever took the kids to the doctor.

Cledia Bertke, 55, Perry County

I remember my brother had stepped on a nail, a rusty nail. My mother said, "Oh, dear," but my grandmother said, "Oh, don't worry about it. Put a piece of salt pork on it." And that's what Mother did. She sliced a piece of pork and put it over where he had that little wound and wrapped it around. I guess it swelled a bit, but after a couple of days he was all right again.

Margaret Larson, Porter County

For swelling, or infected sores or cuts, a good soak in hot water with Epsom salts, and then put a piece of fat meat on the hurt or injury and wrap it up.

Marjorie Malott, 67, Pike County

What would you do it someone stepped on a nail?
We would take ashes from the wood stove and put them in water. The foot was soaked in the water. We used the same method for a smashed finger.

Otillia Buehler, 90, Dubois County

If you run a nail in your foot, [they'd] pour turpentine on it to start with, and it was bandaged up with lye soap and turpentine.

Helen Shockey, 80, Grant County

If you had a cut, to prevent infection she [Mother] would go to the drug store and buy camphor in sort of lumps, like, and then she would take some alcohol and dissolve that camphor in it and put it into a bottle. When you got some of that poured into a cut, I'll tell you, you could see stars, but we never said anything. It was pretty drastic, but I don't think we ever had an infection that I know of.

And that is another thing that Raleigh's had—a liniment that I'm sure was made of red pepper and we got that poured on our sores, but we lived.

Margaret Larson, Porter County

What was your old standby for a cut finger?
Well, usually some kind of cloth wrapped around it.
Let it get well by itself.
Mary Schoen, 93, Floyd County

If you got a sliver in your hand or anything, my Dad always had grafting wax, made with beeswax and mutton tallow. You put that on and it would bring anything out.

Helen Marker, 66, St. Joseph County

I remember I fell on the ice when I was a little child going to school, and sprained my ankle. The remedy then was cider vinegar and salt, and they'd heat it and pour that over my ankle.
Did it work?
Well, I guess it did. I lost three weeks of school, I remember, with it.

Edna Vandenbark, 92, Vanderburgh County

They always got mullein and dried it. If you got a sprain they got it [mullein] hot in vinegar and salt water and that was bound around whatever you had sprained, a foot or whatever.

Helen Shockey, 80, Grant County

EARS

I had the earache so much when I was little and my father would smoke a pipe or a cigar and blow smoke in my ear to loosen up the wax, or something. Then they would steam it with a cup of hot water. We had no aspirin or anything like that in them days and that's what they could do for my earache.
Did it seem to help?
It would help it temporary.

Ozetta Sullivan, 72, Harrison County

My grandmother smoked an old clay pipe. Whenever I had the earache she would fire the old pipe up and blow warm smoke in my ear.
The warm smoke would relieve the earache and she had a salt bag that
they warmed and they put on the ear.

Elizabeth McCullough, 68, Putnam County

My mother would heat a pan of salt, put it in a bag and lay it on my
ear. I suppose it was the heat that made it feel good and that salt
would stay hot a long time. Also, they would fry peach kernels in fresh
lard, then they'd warm that and put a few drops in my ear for earache
when it was real bad. Momma kept peach kernels in the summertime
cooked in that lard to have for my earaches. I know it gave relief, I
guess it was the warmth that did it.

Nellie Frakes, 71, Perry County

I remember Virginia [sister] had the earache when we first came
here. We had the fireplace, and they took the juice out of the green
hickory, they caught that and dropped that in her ear.

I never heard of that one before.

And there was a woman who stayed with us at one time that had a
little boy and he had the earache, and she would often bake onions and
she would take that juice and drop it in his ears for a cure.

Did it really help?

Well, they thought it did, anyway.

Ruth Dye, 75, Martin County

I had an earache an awful lot. I had to walk a mile and half to
school in bad weather, and it was so cold and I'd get earache so much.

Did your mother put anything in your ear?

She used to put a little oil, and she would drop a little warm water in
my ear. But she usually put something in a cloth that was hot. Hot
oats or hot salt, or some kind of material, and I would lay on that ear.
I've often wondered if those earaches weren't the reason I'm so hard of
hearing now.

Pearl Garrison, 92, Carroll County

WARTS

I remember one incident that might be called a folklore cure. I had
a seedy wart on my right hand and it sort of bothered me. We always
had a hired man around. He said he could "pow-wow" it off. So he

rubbed his finger over it and he mumbled some words that I couldn't understand and in three months the wart was gone and it never came back.

Ruth Snyder, 81, Marshall County

Home nursing. Two sisters extract a splinter from a willing victim's foot.
Submitted by Delaware County

I remember rubbing fat meat on warts.

Kathleen Blondia, 65, St. Joseph County

I had warts on my hands and fingers, and I had tried everything, like old dirty dish rags and rubbing old bones on them.

One evening a neighbor that was cutting and shocking corn for my dad came up to the house and he saw the warts on my hand. He looked up at the sun and said, "It is pretty late in the afternoon, but I think your warts will go away." Well, they all disappeared and he didn't even touch them.

Lois Wagoner, 76, Fulton County

Aunt Het Parkhill could and did "take off" warts. The time she took a wart off my finger, she rubbed it in a certain way with a grain of corn which she then put in her apron pocket and refused to tell me what she finally did with the corn. In a few days the wart was gone, leaving no sign it had been there.

Juanita Leech, Crawford County

BOILS

We used to make bread and milk poultices. You could use it for a boil, or to poultice a sore.

What did you put in the bread and milk?

Just bread and milk. Put a little sugar in it so it would help draw. To draw the poison out.

And my husband's mother used to use soap and put sugar in it for a poultice, if you had a boil. Just soap and sugar.

Helen Shockey, 80, Grant County

I had a terrible boil on my chin when I was a girl and poultices of catnip, crushed catnip, were bound on my chin.

Beulah Mardis, 76, Johnson County

What about a sore, or if you had a boil?

Well, they got tar like you put on when you put a wagon wheel on, just plain tar.

Put [that] on a boil?

Yes, or my grandma put a yellow of an egg on a boil. I had one on my chin and I can remember her beating that egg and putting it on.

Mary Foltz, 93, Grant County

Did you use poultices?

My dad used to have boils real bad. They'd put linseed and make a poultice out of it. That would make it draw. He complained about it hurting so bad when they put it on.

I know they wanted red flannel to put a poultice on. I know they saved two or three old flannel dresses. We always saved, kept them clean, so in case somebody needed a poultice, we'd have red flannel to put on their chest.

Edna Maddox, 71, Grant County

One time I remember Mother making mush and putting it on the bottom of my feet. I don't remember my ailment, but I shall never forget that mush oozing between my toes.

Lucile Imes, 82, Noble County

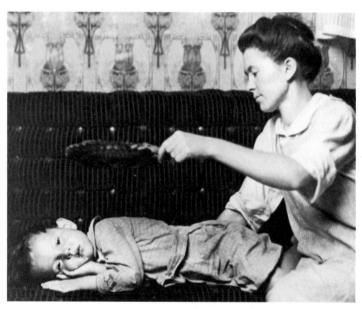

A concerned mother does what she can to help a sick child. Any illness was frightening in this era before modern medical and pharmaceutical discoveries.
Submitted by Whitley County,
L. E. Hoffman, photographer

BURNS

I can remember putting a raw potato on burns.

Mary Ash, 84, Shelby County

As a child I remember they would put soda on burns.

Opal Whitsett, 84, Scott County

My mother always used cotton dipped in kerosene for a burn and

then it would never blister.
Juanita Hunter, 81, Scott County

For burns, an aloe plant.
Juanita Leech, Crawford County

Mother spilled a big pot of hot tea down the front of me one time and we never went to the doctor. She used old black salve and wash rags and put it all over me, and I was fine. We just didn't go to the doctor like today, every time you turn around.
Sharon Windhorst, 35, Fayette County

My father used to, if you burned your finger, he used to go around in a circle and say some secret words. It was supposed to take out the fire, and it worked. My grandmother did it too. He got it from her. I guess he thought, as much as I was always laughing at it, he would never tell me what it was. But, whether it was all in your head or not, it did work.
Barbara Elliott, 54, Wells County

MISCELLANEOUS

You've always heard about the seven-year itch. Well, I got the seven-year itch at school, but I didn't want to tell them [parents]. So I waited until they got it, then I had to say I had it. And I'm sure that my parents was very aggravated at me waiting until they got it before I told them.

The way they doctored it was much different than you'd doctor it now. You put on sulphur and lard at night. We wore long underwear. Then the next morning, you had to get up and take a bath. Well, those times we didn't have a bathroom, and it wasn't as easy to take a bath as it would be now.

Then, afterwards, we found out others at school had it, but nobody said anything.
Catherine Summers, 67, Harrison County

And one time somebody said there was lice in school. Oh, my, Mom and Dad just wore my knees out trying to see if I had any. I had bangs, and Dad found a louse (laughs) in my bangs. I forget what they put on our hair to kill them, but I went to school the next day, and I got to

thinking about it all, and I got sick and went home (laughing). Oh, my!
Cleo Borders, 75, Martin County

I was in a room with first, second, third and fourth graders together.
Impetigo sores were common. One family would not use any medica-
tion or soap on the sores, saying it was not biblical. They had a
number of dogs which licked the sores, because the Bible (according to
them) said to.
Essie Rumble, 77, Gibson County

When I had the toothache, my mother tied bacon onto my jaw. The
bacon would be peppered real good, and that produced heat, and then
when the toothache would stop, I would cry with my skin burning.
Beulah Mardis, 76, Johnson County

. . . and then there was a remedy I always took that my father fixed
for menstrual periods. It was awful good, and it would be good yet
today. I would dig the roots of the black cohosh, they called it. Some
people would call it snakeroot, I expect. We would wash them and dry
them and put them in a bottle of whiskey. A tablespoonful of that
would knock the cramps right now.
Ozetta Sullivan, 72, Harrison County

If we ever got stung with a bee, we just got a bunch of clay and put
on it.
Martha Werner, 63, Franklin County

One time I got bee stung at a neighbors and by the time I got home,
I was about one big welt all over, a-scratching to beat everything. My
mother kept a bottle of whiskey for medicinal purposes, and I suppose
I was the only one of the family that ever got a dose of it, but [that
whiskey] was to kill the poison of the bee sting.
Beulah Rawlings, 76, Hamilton County

My mother-in-law told me, she said, "If a bee stings, take four
weeds." I said, "What kind of weeds?" "It don't make any difference.
Four different kinds of weeds and rub them together till you get a
juice. And rub them on your bee sting and it will take that pain right
out." And it does.
Pearl Hiland, 96, Fulton County

My brother was frail and everyone was worried about him and they
didn't know what to do, but someone came up with the idea of having

him measured. You would take them to someone that understood it, and you'd have to take him so many times and actually be measured with a string, and afterwards you were supposed to watch them gain their health. My brother did get better, but I think that could be attributed to the fact that he had his tonsils removed. After that he was much better.

Gladys Tribolet, 70, Huntington County

COLDS

Used to, didn't have doctors. Doctors would come to the home, but if you just had a little ailment you didn't want to pay for a doctor, because money was too scarce at that time.

What did you do about colds?

Well, we used a mustard plaster on your chest.

How did you make a mustard plaster?

Well, you take mustard and an egg, beat it up.

Is that powdered mustard?

Yes.

How much?

According to how big a poultice you wanted. One or two tablespoons, maybe. Put two tablespoons of flour to each tablespoon of mustard, wet it with hot water and heat it good, put it between rags and put it on your chest and down across your back, for pneumonia.

Helen Shockey, 80, Grant County

Did your mother or any of your family make poultices?

Oh, yes, mustard poultices. I've been blistered with them many times. On my sides and forehead. Yes, I've lived through all of it.

Pearl Garrison, 92, Carroll County

When we got a cold, Mommy fried onions and put some tallow in it, that's tallow from sheep and rubbed the bottom of our feet, and put a poultice on us and put us to bed.

Mary Foltz, 93, Grant County

We used balsam oil. A teaspoon of sugar with a few drops of balsam oil is the method we used. Quinine, turpentine and goose grease was used to rub on chests.

Otillia Buehler, 90, Dubois County

For a real bad cold, we had onion tea, hot onion tea.

That's new. Brewed the tea with onions, and you drank it? What did it taste like?

Oh, not very good.

Did you feel better?

Either better or worse.

Alfreda Wesner, 47, White County

We were always given vinegar for colds. Why, I don't know, but here they come with a tablespoon of vinegar.

My mother was not much to dope. She always said, "Keep the children healthy with good food and warm clothes, and they'll get through."

Eldo Bell, 86, Spencer County

At our house, peppermint was good for anything—colds, flu anything. You took a spoonful of sugar and put a few drops of peppermint on it. When the flu was so bad, when they had the flu epidemic, we were all sick but my dad. Dad was the only one that was up, and that was when peppermint was really used then.

Ellen McAfee, 68, Marshall County

I think maybe my mother stopped the desire for whiskey, because she would always have a remedy when any of us had bad colds. She would take two tablespoons full of sugar and two tablespoons full of whiskey that Papa always kept in the medicine cabinet. She would stir them together and then she would put boiling hot water in on it, in a cup. That would have been real good if it had been nice and cool to drink, but Mom had never tasted it herself yet. She always said, "Here, kid, drink this. It will help your cold."

We drank it so hot that she nearly spoiled my appetite for whiskey when I got to be a young lady.

Did it cure your cold?

Oh, sure, it cured our cold. We jumped all around.

Clara Nichols, 79, Wabash County

What's an onion poultice?

Well, you just cut the onions up and heat them and pound them until it gets real juicy and stick it on their chest. And it's sure to break up pneumonia.

Well, now, is that better than a mustard plaster?

(laughing) Actually, I don't know there's ever been any scientific . . .

(laughing). I often wonder if it wasn't just the heat sort of relieved the congestion.

Neva Schlatter, 79, Pulaski County

There were 13 children in your family. I'm sure you didn't go to the doctor every time you had a cold. Did your mother have anything that she did that you might call a home remedy.

Oh, yes. For colds, she put lard in a pan and sliced onions in it and fry that and, oh, that would smell the whole house up. When you'd go to bed at night, she'd take that and grease it on your chest, put on a flannel rag and pin it to your undershirt. Sometimes it would almost burn you, it was so hot. You would smell that all night and of course you would kind of smell it all the next day, when you went to school. You couldn't wash your undershirt. You didn't have that many undershirts to change.

Dorothy Hoffman, 59, Adams County

My mother always kept a pan of onions and sugar cooking in back of the stove in winter, and we would get some of that juice if we caught cold. We always wore asafetida around our necks. We used pennyroyal tea, soaked our feet in hot water and used a laxative when we caught cold.

Ethel Meyer, 78, Ripley County

The inner bark of slippery elm was used as a poultice on the chest or for infections.

Juanita Leech, Crawford County

SORE THROAT

For sore throats we rubbed on goose grease and tied a stocking around our necks.

Otillia Buehler, 90, Dubois County

If we were sick and had a little sore throat, Mother would put bacon or fat meat around our neck, and a white cloth around it, and we would go to school.

Francis Harley, 89, Marshall County

I've always had sore throats, seemed like. For that they sliced fat meat and put black pepper on it and put a rag around my throat. Seemed like I wore that all the time when I was small.

And then we used to put a few drops of coal oil on sugar for the croup. My goodness, that's all we knew then.
Thelma Fox, 74, Shelby County

For sore throats sometimes you got a cloth saturated with kerosene wrapped around your neck.
Isabel Schoeff, 81, Huntington County

We took our stocking off and turned it wrong side out when we had a sore throat. We'd put the foot of the stocking next to the sore place and wrap it around your neck, fasten it with a safety pin, and slept that way. The next morning your sore throat was gone. I wore that often, because I had a lot of sore throats.

One night Mother greased me with turpentine and some kind of grease and then she laid a warm wool rag on my chest. The next morning, when she took that off, I had blisters from the turpentine. My mother cried, she hated it so.
Alma Knecht, 78, Wabash County

Did your mother have a certain thing if you had a sore throat?
Oh, boy, did she! You was greased with Vicks Salve and then you took your long stocking off with the foot of it around the sore part of your throat, and wrapped around your throat and fastened with a safety pin. I never knew what that had to do with it, but usually you were up without a sore throat the next morning. But I did get a clean pair of stockings.
Opal Gallagher, 72, Shelby County

My aunt told me about using beets for sore throat or tonsillitis. Grind them up, raw beets, and heat them and put them between cloths and put them around your neck. I always used beets for my kids.
Helen Shockey, 80, Grant County

Did you ever have egg poultices for your sore throat? You take the yellow of an egg and fill it with salt and then put it on a piece of cloth, double the cloth so it's not gonna burn you, then you can wear it. It draws [the soreness] out.
Valetta Ford, 69, Randolph County

If we had a sore throat, or a scratchy throat, my mother had a glass jar which had powdered sulphur in it, and she also had a little glass tube that was about six inches long. She would dip that into the sulphur and get some of it into that tube. Then one end of the tube was stuck down in my throat and she was on the other end and blew that stuff down my throat. It didn't taste very good, but I guess it did the job. I used to hate it, but that was the way it was.

Elsie Nickel, Porter County

Gargling with salt water—a home remedy.
J. C. Allen Collection

The remedy we had was even worse. One of the neighbors told Mother to take a spoon and put some sugar in it and one drop of kerosene. I went many days with a terrible sore throat before I would tell

Mother I had one [sore throat], to avoid that. But I guess it was all right.

Margaret Larson, Porter County

Hot salt water was the gargle for sore throats. That is a good one yet today.

Marjorie Malott, 67, Pike County

I can remember my mother using that old bad-tasting liniment and swabbing my throat.

Virlee Jochum, 64, Dubois County

COUGHS

There was an old man in Lisbon who did trapping and hunting during the winter months. His specialty was skunk grease. It was light yellow and a consistency of cold cream. It was made from the fat of skunks. [When] the winter came, Mother would always get a bottle of skunk oil. I think she probably paid 25 or 30 cents for it. And at the very first sign of croup, I was always rubbed with the oil and a flannel cloth placed over my chest. It was a sure cure.

Lucile Imes, 82, Noble County

We got onion cough syrup when we had a cough. You would take the onions and slice them and sprinkle sugar over them and let them sit overnight and they would form a syrup. You would be given this syrup for your cough.

Beulah Grinstead, 68, Hamilton County

My grandpa used to get rock candy and whiskey and put glycerin in it and let it set until the rock candy dissolved. He used it for cough syrup.

Ruth Dane, 81, Madison County

We used to take horehound candy and make cough syrup out of it. Put lemon juice in the horehound candy.
You made your own cough drops?
Well, it was syrup after you put the lemon juice in it.

Helen Shockey, 80, Grant County

Mom always, every fall, she would be beginning to prepare medicine for winter. Dad would go out and dig wild cherry roots and she would take just little pieces of it and she would put water with it and she would boil it down real low.

I don't remember if she put anything in with it, but that is what we used for cough medicine and it always helped.

And then another remedy she had, she would get whiskey and rock candy and a little bit of sugar and a little bit of water. And that was really good (laughs) for a cough.

Cleo Borders, 75, Martin County

And Grandma made cough syrup, because you couldn't trust what you bought, she didn't think.

What was in Grandma's cough syrup? What did it taste like?

It had a taste like the cough syrups that we get today. I can't remember the name of what Grandma bought and put in it.

Did she leave you any recipe?

No, cause Grandma had it all out of her head.

Edna Winter, 74, Pulaski County

When I had a cold she mixed up some horrible stuff with licorice, crystal candy and honey, I believe, and I don't know what else, but it was horrible. She made it in a quart jar like you can in, and I would have to take a tablespoon every time I coughed.

Evelyn Buchanan, 78, Scott County

We used honey and lemon juice for cough medicine. The honey might be from our own bees that we had on the farm.

Sarah Amstutz, 81, DeKalb County

I like to mix up my own medicine. Now it doesn't always work, and I sometimes end up going to the doctor, but if I have a real, real severe sore throat and I just can't hardly talk—well, I like to make fresh lemon juice and lots of sugar, and whiskey. I put this on top of the stove and I make this just as hot as I can stand it. We supped this out of a teaspoon and, seriously, that really has helped a lot of people (laughs).

But I'm laughing because we don't drink and to go into a liquor store and buy your whiskey, that is the hardest part.

Mary Ann Haskins, 49, Grant County

STOMACHACHE AND DIARRHEA

My grandmother had lots of indigestion through the years, and her cureall for that was baking soda and water. She added boiling water to the baking soda, and when I'd walk into her apartment, I'd hear the teakettle boiling.

Judi Merkel, 34, Adams County

My grandmother used to have a cure of sugar and whiskey for a stomachache.

Mary Smoker, 64, Kosciusko County

For stomachache, you take hot water, a little sugar and a drop of liniment. Did you ever hear of that?

Evelyn Koehler, 68, St. Joseph County

If we had kind of a queasy stomach, she [Mother] would give us essence of peppermint that she bought at the drugstore. She would add a little water and a little bit of sugar.

Elsie Nickel, Porter County

For a sick stomach, my mother always took the new growth on a peach tree and boiled it, and we drank peach tea.

Juanita Hunter, 81, Scott County

Mother had balsam apples, and you poured whiskey on those, and that was a good remedy for stomach troubles. One time it kept disappearing, this whiskey she made, and she had to replace it all the time. Come to find out, the hired hand had gotten into it.

Thelma Robeson, 71, Fayette County

For diarrhea, blackberry juice.

Juanita Leech, Crawford County

I saw Mom take whiskey, put it in a saucer and light it, so it would burn itself off and leave some liquid. [That was] for diarrhea.

Cledia Bertke, 55, Perry County

At Christmas or Easter—anytime there had been more candy, more sweets, more cakes—then we had to have a dose of syrup of pepsin before we went to bed. Without fail, this is what ended the day.

Sarah Witham, 40, Dearborn County

ASAFETIDA

I wore an asafetida bag around my neck to school to keep off diseases, and I did that 'til I was married.

Edna Vandenbark, 92, Howard County

They bought the asafetida in the drug stores and they just got about ten cents worth, and they'd put it in a little rag, and they'd sew it up and they'd get a grocery string and tie it around your neck and send you to school.

It [asafetida] looked like a piece of candy, a little square like. I think of those little oat things in cereal, make me think [of it]. It's a terrible smell, and you wrap it in a little rag and put it around your neck when you're little. Of course, everybody smells alike. It's worse than garlic.

Mary Foltz, 89, Grant County

I always kind of felt that asafetida kept your friends away, and that's the reason you weren't contaminated.

Edna Maddox, 71, Grant County

It was against my religion (laughs). I never did like to wear it and Mom said, "You have to wear it, you just have to wear it."

Cleo Borders, 75, Martin County

We had to wear asafetida around our necks that we had to wear to school all winter. When the schoolroom got warm, I tell you, it was not like a bee in a bed of roses, standing around the stove with asafetida.

My sister one time told me that she and her friend took their string off and tied it on to a bush by the toilet and then went into school and said they didn't have to wear it. But she said it didn't do any good, because everyone had it on and you could smell it all over the schoolhouse.

Alvah Watson, 97, Allen County

DRINKS, TEAS AND SPRING TONICS

My brother and I in the spring, as soon as the garlic would come up, we would have to eat a little of that garlic, because it was good for youngsters.

We both despised it. I don't even use garlic about my cooking. I don't use a bit of garlic. I don't even like to hear the word mentioned. I can still remember exactly where it grew in the garden.

Pearl Garrison, 92, Carroll County

There were different things good for spring tonic.

Yes, wild greens! And that was something I didn't care for, but we had them because my mother loved them. My father ate them, but he'd make an awful face while he was eating them. He'd eat them because he knew they were good for him.

Ruth Dye, 75, Martin County

And then in the spring they'd give us molasses and sulphur. We always had a lot of sorghum molasses.

And that's a spring tonic?

Oh, yeah, sulphur and molasses.

Mary Foltz, 93, Grant County

In the spring, we had to drink sassafras. My mother believed in it. I don't know where she came up with it. I reckon she grew up with it. In the spring, we would always drink sassafras tea. Why, that thins your blood.

Pearl Garrison, 92, Carroll County

Sassafras tea—my dad [used it] to settle his stomach, and then you'd breathe in the vapors from the tea, that opened up your sinuses, so it was kind of a cure-all.

It was rather good, but a little bit of sassafras tea goes a long way. It's not something you want day in and day out.

Judi Merkel, 34, Adams County

Grandma Carlin knew a lot of things, too. She made tea out of sassafras, spice wood tea and dandelion tea.

Stella Irwin, 84, Parke County

Peppermint used to grow wild down in the bottom of the back fields. We used to go out and pick it, then she would wash [the leaves] and dry them. When we were sick she would pour hot water over them and give that to us, with a little sugar, as tea.

Mary Schoen, 93, Floyd County

My mother gathered a lot of tea leaves in the summer, pennyroyal, and then there was always mint. It grew along the fence rows. We would gather our supply for winter. I had a lot of sick headaches when I was young. I would have it and I would throw up. Could not keep anything on my stomach for two or three days. Then I would have to drink pennyroyal tea.

Did you like the tea?

Well, it wasn't bad. Put a little sugar in it. Don't like to see penny-royal yet today.

Pearl Garrison, 92, Carroll County

Then we had peach leaf tea. My grandmother used to brew that up when she was just really bad. If you were sick, you were bound to get better, because it was so awful you would get better, just because you could not stand to drink it.

Barbara Elliott, 54, Wells County

There were some things we used to collect and they were weeds, really, wild weeds. I remember one in particular. It was called cham-omile. That was wonderful for sore throat and also that was used if you had a fever.

If we had flu we were stuck in bed and we would have to drink that tea, hot chamomile tea, and we were made to sweat, perspire. We were covered up with feather beds and we had to stay under that until we just sweat up a storm, until that fever broke.

Terry Fecher, 50, Rush County

We used to have all kind of old remedies. You know that mullein that grows out—well, [brew it] with a little cinnamon and a little cloves, and make a tea. That was good.

Grace Hawkins, 93, Martin County

Mother would make tea. For babies she'd make catnip tea—catnip grew out in our garden. We had two big plants of sage in our garden, and sometimes [she would] make sage tea.

Mary Gleason, 87, Perry County

What about when babies were small and had the colic. What did they do for something like that?

We used catnip tea for my babies. We grew our own catnip, and that is about the only thing we ever did for colic.

Did you sweeten it?

Yes, we sweetened it.

Did it work?
Yes, either that or something else, but we thought it was that.
Opal Whitsett, 84, Scott County

When we got sick there was the thing—in Swiss we called it Epsha tea. I'm not sure what the English name would be.
No matter what you had—if you were sick at your stomach, you got the tea. If you had a headache, you got the tea. The thing about it was—it always made you throw up. That's the reason you got better.
This was a tea that [your mother] brewed?
Yes, it had a little white flower and we always got it at our neighbor's, Mrs. Enos Lehman. She had it in her backyard. In English maybe it was just a weed, I don't know. It was a terrible tasting tea.
Sarah Zeigler, 53, Adams County

And if the kids got sick, we took Castoria.
What is Castoria?
It's to physic you, that's a laxative. They used to think a laxative would cure just about anything.
Mary Foltz, 93, Grant County

Sage and senna tea was used as a laxative.
Juanita Leech, Crawford County

And they would put in castor oil in orange juice. That just turned me off. It has a terrible taste. I don't like oranges on that account.
Grace Hawkins, 93, Martin County

I took lots and lots of castor oil as a girl! I couldn't take it the way everybody was supposed to. We would stop at the drug store, and Dad would have a soda fixed up with castor oil in it.
I'll always remember one night we brought my grandmother home with us. I'd been sick all day, and Dad had decided it was time for the castor oil treatment. So we stopped and he got the soda fixed up and brought it out to the car. I can still hear Grandma Baker say, "I want one, too." Dad looked her in the eye and said, "No, you don't."
Alice Gentry, 68, Hamilton County

Did you have to take castor oil?
No, but I gave it to my boy. I guess that is why he grew up to have so much courage.
Pearl Garrison, 92, Carroll County

PATENT
MEDICINES

The one I remember was if we got a bad cold and had a chest congestion, she [mother] would always rub us with Vicks Salve and take a flannel rag and make it warm and put it on our chest and sent us to bed.

Did it work?

Well, it sure relieved the congestion if you breathed that Vicks Salve in your nose. I don't know if it really helped that much, but it seemed to at the time.

Dorothy Fuhrman, 40, Martin County

My mother, if I would take a cold, she would rub my chest with Vicks Salve. She always made a little thing—kind of like a bib—[that she could pull up] tight on you, and it wouldn't loosen up. She put the Vicks on and then that bib on.

Gaby Moon, 69, Clay County

My girls, even after they got big, big enough to be runnin' around, they would come home at night with a sore throat and hoarse. I'd wait until they went to sleep and grease them with Vicks Salve. It would make them so mad.

Valetta Ford, 69, Randolph County

I don't think we had a doctor much. We just did it ourselves with hot drinks and Vicks Salve. Vicks Salve is one of my main medicines. I feel like a lot of times that saved our life. Now the doctors don't believe in that, but I sure do. I just feel like I couldn't have raised my family if it hadn't been for Vicks Salve.

Florence LaGrange, 79, Perry County

Mother believed in lots of Vicks Salve rubbed on chest and back. As I talk about this, I can almost feel her hands, rubbing me so gently.

Mary Ann Moore, 57, Hendricks County

When Bob first started school, he had stepped on a thorn. He came home and he told me about it. Well, I bathed his foot good and put a bandage around it, then I soaked that good with a remedy that we

used to always have in the house. I don't know whether you can even
find it in the drugstore any more, but it was called Hamlen's Wizard
Oil. That got all right without any soreness at all. That was a great
remedy in those times. We always had it in the house.

Iva Crouse, 85, White County

There were two kinds of patent medicine that we always kept on
hands. One was called "World's Benefactor." It was something on the
order of sweet oil. The other was a "summer complaint" medicine. Oh,
it was just as hot as fire, but if you'd get cramps or diarrhea, it was
good.

Maggie Owen, 95, Whitley County

Well, the Raleigh man lived in Valparaiso and he came out in the
country with his horse and buggy. He was very welcome. It was kind
of fun to have them come and they tried to talk our parents into buying this, that and the other. We had Raleigh yellow salve, Raleigh
vanilla, Raleigh cinnamon, Raleigh cloves, and Raleigh disinfectant.

The disinfectant came in gallon cans like you buy oil in now. They
were square cans with a spout in the end. My father had typhoid fever
once and I can remember that Mother put it [disinfectant] in the water
and scrubbed everything every day with Raleigh disinfectant.

It smelled like carbolic acid, and I think, probably a lot of that was
in it. It was also used in the hen house to make that clean and sanitary.
It was used in the barn and in the calf stall and for anything that
needed disinfecting or sterilizing.

There was also the Watkins man, and there are still Watkins men
around yet.

And then there was a man by the name of Kurito Sven. He was
Clarence Johnson's father and he sold this tonic Kurito which was
good for anything. Every last Swede in Baillytown and Porter had a
bottle of Kurito.

Margaret Larson, Porter County

There was one liniment that was just the greatest thing—it almost
cured everything. That was Black Diamond liniment. Some people
called it Barbed Wire Liniment, and some called it Horse Liniment. It
really would cure just about anything.

Ruth Bateman, 63, Daviess County

We've come a long way since then, haven't we?
Yes. Now they just give you some shots.

Bessie Werner, 80, Pulaski County

GROWING UP
IN MY COMMUNITY

"We had a happy childhood and a happy young life.
It was altogether different than it is today,
because we didn't get very far from home.
The church and the school were the
social contacts at the time we were growing up."

Zelma Blocher, 81, Scott County

A Sunday evening picnic with the young
people of the neighborhood.
Submitted by Rush County

HELPING
EACH OTHER

Our neighbors were really friendly with each other. When you got
your work done and the others needed help, everybody went in and
helped them. If they had problems in the family and needed help, all
the neighbors would go and take their tools and help each other out,
and the women would fix dinner for them.
  Elma Matthew, 74, Madison County

Whenever any of the neighbor men would get sick, the neighbors
would all pitch in. They'd go and help put out the crops, or help to
gather them in, or whatever needed doing. If the women would get
down sick, we'd go in and take them things and help out every which
way we could. It's a good friendly neighborhood out there.
  Masa Scheerer, 82, Huntington County

They all worked together all the time. There was a neighbor north of
us that their son had diphtheria. He finally died; he was about ten years
old at that time.
  The neighbors did the chores and my brother set on the porch, just
to be near them, because no one could go in the house.
  Lois Wagoner, 76, Fulton County

When somebody was sick, we had no hospital here—and the men
always came and sat up at night.
  Hilda Thomas, 83, Jackson County

When there was sickness in the neighborhood, we always liked to go
and help out. Take a dish of food. And I still hardly go anywhere
where I don't take a pie or a plate of cookies. I just love to do that.
There is always a need for help from others. This is what I learned long
ago. If I can be of service to other people this is what I like to do. It is
very rewarding to me.
  Alma Knecht, 78, Wabash County

Sometimes our neighbors would have a lot of, say, potatoes and
we'd have a lot of, say, sweet potatoes. Then we'd switch back and
forth, so both would have.
  And if you went away, to a neighbors, you wouldn't lock up. They

never locked the houses, but they never lost anything. You were more apt to find someone had been there and left something on the table for you when you got back.

Alvah Watson, 97, Allen County

They had horse thief associations. When anything suspicious occurred in the night—it didn't have to be horse stealing, it could be something else—members were alerted by telephone and then they would establish a road block at certain points. To establish the road block and to justify trying to stop somebody, there was a banner which was made of oilcloth—maybe three feet by five feet. This gave a member of the chapter substance, and this gave you the authority to stop somebody. If conditions warranted, you could hold them until some law officer could come. You had no power to arrest; the power was investigative.

There were at least four of these horse thief associations in the county. They had badges—I remember the one that said The Africa Detective Association. Africa was the name given to the South Liberty area; the school, the church and the community.

There are stories of rustlers driving horses into centralized areas; painting the blazes off the face; or painting white feet off; then driving them into Ohio and selling them. One of the rallying points was supposedly down in Jackson Township.

Fred Park, 74, Wells County

We had fire brigades. If there was a fire in the community, the telephone rang five times and everybody grabbed a bucket and went to help put out the fire.

Mary Dean, 76, Clinton County

We had a party line and they used to send out the fire alarm on the party lines. They would ring ten or more rings, real fast, to [have people pick up the phone] and tell where the fire was.

It was an all-volunteer fire department, and they needed everybody's help, and that's how they would send out the fire alarm. Anybody and everybody would go and see if they could help.

Dora Giggy, 79, Lagrange County

Our grandfather made sorghum molasses. It was a great community occasion. Several neighbors raised a small patch of sorghum. They all brought it to our grandfather's. He had a vat under an open shed to boil the sweet juice. A mill was horse-turned to squeeze the juice into a ½ barrel which was poured into the cooker. It was cooked and skimmed most of the day, starting very early in the morning. This was done in the fall so the days were short and the air crisp and pretty cool. Most of the neighbors were there to help and visit. Most of the children in the neighborhood would gather after school and someone would whittle small wood paddles for each to taste the cooked molasses. The women of the neighborhood would peel apples and when the molasses was finished, the apples were poured into the vat with some cider and they made delicious apple butter. Then it was divided and everyone went home, usually after dark. It was a great occasion.

Bea Shuel, 75, Gibson County

Can you think of other instances when neighbors helped each other out?

They used to do it for butchering. They would get together early in the morning. The men would kill the hogs and get them into the boiling water and as they cut up the animals the women would work on making the sausage and things like that.

Dora Giggy, 79, Lagrange County

When you butchered, did you divide with your neighbors?

Oh, goodness yes. They always took a piece of fresh meat home with them and then when they butchered, we helped them and we got fresh meat back. And if you had garden stuff, you gave some to them and then they would give you back later on. Whatever the neighbors had, you would have, too.

Juanita: It was a time of sharing.

Opal: Back then it seemed like everybody was a friend to everybody.

Opal Whitsett, 84, and Juanita Hunter, 81, Scott County

What were events when the whole neighborhood helped?

They helped one another an awful lot. They helped one another farm; they helped one another thresh; they would cut corn for fodder; they would butcher; they would cut ice together; they helped every way.

Bessie Werner, 80, Pulaski County

If you went to raise a barn, all of the farmers would come and join in that. Maybe two or three days they would work there, putting up the barn.

Audry Blackburn, 86, Posey County

We just lived a mile from the colored settlement when I was growing up. This was Roberts Chapel and it was originally French-Indian people, the whole settlement, but they finally became mixed with the Negroes. I went to school with them and we got along fine. In fact, when I was an eighth grader, my best friend was a Negro girl. My dad sang with the Roberts Chapel quartet on many different occasions. Most often with Wash Cotton, the neighbor who lived a mile from us. He had a very deep bass and my dad loved to sing with him.

So the Ku Klux Klan came along and they tried to get my dad to join. But he came home and said, "I'll not join that. They're against the Negro. These Negroes are my friends. I make hay with them; I fill silos with them; I eat in their houses; they eat in mine; they're my friends. I'm not going to join anything like that." So then he would have no part of it.

Beulah Grinstead, 68, Hamilton County

When they had quilting bees all the ladies came to work on the quilt. Now whose quilt was it?

You were invited to the hostess' home to help quilt [her quilt]. They'd have a pitch-in dinner and just a social event, and work on the quilt. And maybe that day somebody would say, "Well, now, I want you to come to my house next week."

Then she'd be the hostess and serve [and work on her quilt].

That's right. Oh, that was a lot of fun. We enjoyed working on the quilts.

Eula Kelso, 78, Lawrence County

Everybody helped each other as much as they could. They didn't ask for money, or wouldn't take any if you offered it to them.

Edna Klinstiver, 58, Floyd County

What do you remember about threshing dinners and neighbors doing things back and forth together?

Oh, I remember the FEEDS that we fixed. My mother cooked two meals a day for the threshers when they were there . . . Oh, we had sumptuous meals. My mother always baked pie, there was cake, generally beef and noodles, that always went well, and mashed potatoes, and all the different kinds of vegetables that came from the garden. She was a good cook. She baked marvelous bread. I can't remember what the neighbor ladies' specialty was, but my mother's was the bread. Her bread could compare to some people's angel food cake! It was delicious. She made about . . . I suppose she averaged 24 loaves a week. Besides the cakes and pies and rolls and cookies, but then there were "umpteen" of us to eat.

You are talking about 24 loaves, not counting threshing day, this was a normal week?

That was a NORMAL week! The neighbor ladies would change, just like the men would change help at threshing time. My mother would go and help other ladies, and then they would come help her. And of course, us kids always got wrung in on that helping, too. I can remember pumping two tubs of water for the men to wash in when they got through threshing, and then hanging out all those towels, and putting out the soap. We had one neighbor man, he came while I was doing this, he came up for a drink of water. He said, "What are we having for dinner today?" So I started telling him, and he said "Having pie?" "Oh, yes,Mom baked pie this morning," I said. "What kind did she bake? There's only two kinds I like." Then I was worried that maybe she baked some kind he didn't like. I started telling him, "Fresh cherry pie, why?" He said, "Oh, I only like hot pie and cold pie!" (laughter)

How many men, on an average, would you have to feed at threshing time?

Oh, I suppose we'd have 10-15 men.

A lot of extra mouths . . . in addition to the family members.

Yes, yes; we always fed the men first and got them out of the way, then the ladies and us kids ate.

Bernice Esch, 70, Lagrange County

My experience with threshing dinners was when I visited my grandparents in the summertime. They had what they called a threshing ring because everybody didn't have a combine or threshing outfit of their own back then. Whenever you had the threshing ring at your house, you provided the dinner for all the people and all the women in the community whose husbands were working with the threshing ring would come in and help get the dinner. They didn't have facilities for keeping food overnight, so the chickens were dressed in the morning, the pies were baked that morning, and everybody would come and they each had a job to do.

We probably started about seven o'clock in the morning and got everything ready. Sometimes, there would be fifteen to twenty-five men, and the women and all the children went, so it was a big day! Then in the afternoon, after all the work was done, the children got to go out and play and the women sat around and talked and visited and caught up on all the latest gossip.

Helen Musselman, 68, Hamilton County

As I look back, we almost felt our neighbors were a family. There was such a closeness. If anything happened at a neighbors, my parents would go over; and if anything happened here, the neighbors would come.

Audry Blackburn, 86, Posey County

Were they more neighborly than they are now?
Very neighborly. Everybody in town knew everybody else. They were all on an equal. Even those who had means were not any different than those who didn't have very much.

Bernice Hirst, 87, Lagrange County

Threshing time was a hot, dusty work-filled event, but it was marked by the friendly neighborliness of small close-knit communities. Children remember the glorious threshing dinners.
Submitted by Grant County

It used to be in this block, I mean the whole block, we knew each other and we would visit back and forth. We would do things for them. We would know what they were doing, and if they needed something, we'd do it. Like care for the children or if they were going to have company we'd fix something for them. And the children all played together. They would have a real good time. We don't have that at all any more.

Donna Parker, 83, Wayne County

I remember one of the neighborhood things, in growing up. All our neighbors took time to take out a day or two for picnics. We'd go to Oliver Lake, which had no cottages then, just tall grass. We would lay out a tablecloth on the grass, and we'd have potato salad and fried chicken and biscuits, just picnic food. But we made time to spend together as a neighborhood.

And in the winter we would go, each week, to one or another neighbor's home for an oyster supper, or some special meal. It would be an evening of a good supper and a lot of fun and games for the children, and visiting, or playing checkers for the men.

We were really close. When one neighbor was hurting, the others always pitched in, in whatever way was necessary, to help. You always had someone who would come if you needed help.

Ruth Hostetler, 79, Lagrange County

Whether it was wedding, or deaths, or threshing, or butchering, we all got together and helped each other.

Maud Sloneker, 90, Fayette County

SHOPPING

We had peddlers. They'd come around with their wares. They were foreigners. They would be selling little trinkets like thimbles or needles—all different gadgets. Sometimes they would have things Mother said she never saw before, those peddlers going through the country.

Alvah Watson, 97, Allen County

There were peddlers who came through the country a lot of time and you didn't even know them. There was [a peddler] one, they called him Indiana, but his name was McGinley. He was a little Irishmen. He would come up here and stay in the country the whole winter. A lot of time he would stay at Mom and Dad's for six weeks if the weather would get bad. My dad would take care of his horse.

And you didn't think about charging him, either.

Oh, you didn't charge him anything. No, they were just delighted when they would see him come. Just tickled to death to see him. He always went to Mom's mother and dad, too. He must have been 150 (laughs).

Cleo Borders, 75, Martin County

We had two hucksters. One was from Mt. Etna and one was from Bancoe. One came one day and the other another day. They would go from house to house and they'd have their wagons with beans and sugar and coffee. They'd have dry goods, maybe gingham or calico. Underneath they'd have a box to put chickens. And on the other side they'd hang a little tank they'd put coal oil [kerosene] in. One time my mother sent me to borrow eggs, so she would have enough to pay for what the huckster was to bring her that day.

Alvah Watson, 97, Allen County

The huckster wagon or truck brought groceries and merchandise to the doors of rural families.
Submitted by White County

We bought most of our groceries off a huckster wagon. Sometimes if we didn't have the money, we would sell some of our chickens to get what we wanted.

The huckster would come by, and we would put our basket out on the mail box and get our bread. I don't think we paid over 9 to 10 cents. There really wasn't much to buy. We had our own meat and garden produce; we had our own milk and butter.

Did they have stores like today?

They had stores. When we came to Rising Sun, we came to the

A & P store to get our flour. Mr. Galbreath had a little grocery store
at North's landing that we did quite a bit of trading. We first got our
mail there—we didn't have a mail route. That was a treat, to go get
groceries and maybe get some candy.

Clara Ashcraft, 70, Ohio County

We didn't make any long trips, too far to go on a long trip in a
buggy or surrey. Oh, we would go once or twice a year to Greensburg,
and once or twice a year to North Vernon. We'd go early of a morning,
unhitch our horses and tie them to a rack somewhere, take some horse
feed along, hay or corn, something. Then we'd spend the day shopping.
We did it in the spring and the fall.

Lennie Hern, 90, Decatur County

On Saturday it was always a treat to drive in to Scottsburg. They
[parents] would go in the morning and park the car—they had a tour-
ing car—and they would go to the grocery and buy crackers, cheese
and bologna. They would eat that at noon, and then Father would do
the shopping and they would come back home.

Evelyn Buchanan, 78, Scott County

Mother went to the grocery store once a week and that was Saturday night, when everything was done, because my father said he
couldn't farm Main Street! (laughs)
**You said the stores were open until 11:00 p.m. Evidently a lot of
farmers did that.**
Yes, and there used to be band concerts on Saturday nights, and
we'd go in for that. We'd all clean up, ready for bed, and then we'd get
in the car and go up and listen to the band, the whole family.

Bernice Esch, 70, Lagrange County

If we had to go shopping, like to buy a new dress, Harrison had
quite a few shops there. They had a drygoods store and just about anything people in the country needed.
But I remember one time, when I was a child, of going to Cincinnati
to do some shopping and we went to a ten cent store. It had two
floors—one floor up some steps—and they had all kinds of things.
And I bought a penny ring. It had a set in it. I thought that was the
greatest thing, when I bought that ring. I must have been about seven
or eight years old.

Thelma Nixon, 68, Union County

I can remember Grandma Miller running a small grocery with candy and things like that. I can remember going over there. If I only had a penny, I would buy me a penny's worth of candy. They would measure it out in a little small glass.

Measure the candy?

Yes, so much candy you got for a penny. They weren't price-marked. They was small candies—smaller than M & M's are today. I know one time she game me a little glass [like they measured in] and I was really thrilled.

A grocery store of the 1900s, with cans on
shelves behind the counter and scales
and a coffee grinder in the foreground.
Indiana State Historical Library

I used to love to go over there, because Grandma Miller was a real typical Grandma. She wore the long dresses and big aprons, too.

Thelma Roehr, 69, Posey County

I remember when I was a child, my mother would give me a quarter, 25¢, and I would go and get 25¢ worth of steak, beefsteak, and that was enough for our whole family.

For the five children and your parents?

Yes. We bought our eggs from the store, but the farmers had

brought the eggs in [to pay for their groceries]. There were several people around town that had cows, and we always bought milk from the people in town. It wasn't pasteurized. We used to take a little pail over and get a quart or two quarts of milk. I have no idea about the price.

Bernice Hirst, 87, Lagrange County

One thing we liked to do as children was pick up the Sears and Roebuck catalog and we'd choose what we liked on each page. She

Trips to town in a horse and buggy were infrequent, but were a real event.
Submitted by Madison County

[sister] would point to something that she liked and then I would point to something I liked. We had fun doing that.

Did your parents order stuff from Sears?

Yes, they did quite a bit of their shopping in the mail order catalogs.

Thelma Nixon, 67, Union County

And we got the Sears Roebuck general catalog. That was something else. You could just spend day after day looking at it. And when the catalog was old, my sister and I could have it to play with. They had watches, men's watches, life size with pictures of birds and flowers and animals. We used to cut them out and pin them on [us] you know. Putting them on was big entertainment. And the ladies in the catalog were our paper dolls. And they had pictures of harness displayed on horses. That was good because we could have horses to race with.

Elsie Nickel, Porter County

MAIL

What did you have to bring in the news?
Well Grandma took a Chicago paper. We went to Grandma's and picked up the paper after it was a day old. And there was a gossip bench at the little grocery store a mile down the road. They always went every night. The post office was there and you'd get the mail and pick up the neighborhood news.

Edna Winter, 74, Pulaski County

We had a post office that was four miles away. They took the mail in once a week. And we would go there on a Saturday and get the mail for the neighborhood. Then we'd take it to a central house—take our mail out and then take it over there.

Then maybe next week it's be their turn to get the mail. They'd always go on horseback and go over and get the mail. The mail routes hadn't started yet when we left the farm.

Alvah Watson, 97, Allen County

The first post office I remember was when I was a very young girl. We had our post office in the Gary Long building. There was a grocery store and a variety store and, in this one corner, was our post office. It was run by an elderly lady. We had different boxes, and we would have to go up to the window and she would hand us our mail.

I wasn't too much in favor of home delivery [when it came] because I loved to walk to the post office.

Eulalia Slater, 63, Porter County

We did have rural mail delivery, but not right to the front of the house, as it is nowadays. If you lived on a main road, you were lucky, for then you could just walk out to the road in front of your house and pick up the mail from the mail box there.

But we lived ¾ of a mile west of the Michigan road on a little-traveled road, so our mail box was out by the side of the Michigan Road along with two others, and someone had to walk that ¾ of a mile and then back if we got our mail.

As my dad took a daily Chicago newspaper and he liked to read some of the news after he ate his dinner, someone usually went after it during the forenoon, and that was someone was quite often a little girl named Ruth. I really didn't mind it too much if I hadn't been so terribly afraid of snakes. I can only remember seeing one once, but anyway, I was afraid I would.

Ruth Snyder, 83, Marshall County

In 1918, the river froze over and our mail came from West Point, Ky., so they had to bring the mail across walking. They carried a long pole with them, because if the ice broke through with them, they could always put the pole out and [it would hold them].

That was still dangerous, because the current . . .

Yes, it was dangerous, but that was the only way. Life was dangerous in lots of things in those days. I have a picture of my dad taken on the frozen river with his long pole.

Catherine Summers, 67, Harrison County

GYPSIES AND TRAMPS

When we lived out along the river, there was an open spot back off the road, right along the river, like a little clearing. When I was little, the gypsies used to come down there every summer and park.

They used to come up to our house. My dad would say, "Well, they are going to come and steal a couple of chickens. While they are asking to buy some eggs, they are stealing four chickens."

I was fascinated with the gypsies. They had wagons then. They would stay there for a couple of weeks and camp down there and fish in the river. My mother would say, "Never go down there," and as soon as she said it, I was gone.

They would talk very broken English and I was just fascinated. They would laugh, and they used to have a banjo or a guitar they used to play, and they would sing. They were so different; they were like something I had never seen.

Barbara Elliott, 54, Wells County

Can you tell us about your experience with gypsies?
Yes. This was when we lived near the church house, a half mile from our house. That [church] made an ideal camping ground for gypsies because there was space to park. They drove in caravans of horses with covered wagons and they had their pots and pans hanging on the outside. So this church house would have a place for them to park; also, they could have water [from the church pump] and the outside toilets which they needed.

So there they would park and at night they would go out and get their food for the next day—which would be your chickens out of your chicken coops and your eggs, if you had any out there. And in your garden, they would pick your vegetables. That was how they would get their food.

So then they took the chicken feathers and dyed them beautiful colors and made flowers out of them. Then they would come around to your house and sell you your chicken feathers made into a flower. But they were really pretty.

Did you have a fear of these gypsies?
Oh, yes, we did. We were always warned never to go with them, because they kidnapped children.

Also, the grocery stores only had one clerk in the store, and they would go in the store and one member would keep the clerk busy while the others would roam around the store and pick up little things and put them in their dresses which was large blouses and skirts where they could stuff things. They would steal out of the stores that way.

Ellen McAfee, 68, Marshall County

During the summer lots of times pack peddlers and transients would walk through the country. For some reason they would stop at our house and my daddy was always kind to them. He'd give them something to eat and then if it was near night he would give them a lantern and open the door to the schoolhouse and let them spend the night there. He was always the janitor of the schoolhouse.

Beulah Grinstead, 68, Hamilton County

You've talked about your father taking people into your home. Do you remember tramps or bums would come to your door during the Depression?
No one was ever turned away.

A lot of times these bums would come and ask if there was wood they could split to pay for a meal. Sometimes there was, sometimes there wasn't. Even so, my folks would always say, "Sit down on the porch and we'll bring you something."

Only once did anybody ever turn up their nose. Mother had just baked bread and that was all she had just then. She buttered him up a nice piece of bread and put apple butter on it. She fixed it up real nice for him, and she told him that was all she had. He walked off, we watched, and he threw it down alongside the road. Evidently he wasn't too hungry.

Bernice Esch, 70, Lagrange County

And my people were always the kind that were taking someone in and even the tramps who came to the door and wanted a bite to eat. I remember one night, it was cold and snowy, somebody knocked at the door. We were all sitting in the living room, Dad went to the door and here was a great huge man, whiskers all over his face, and he said, "Can I come in and get warm and will you keep me for the night?" Dad looked at him and he said "I haven't a bed empty in the house but" he said "if you want to sleep down by the furnace, I'll make you a bed on the hot air box down there and you will be warm." He said "I'll do it." So Dad let him in. We children were all frightened to death when we saw him. I can see that man yet and the next morning we woke up the first thing Mother said she thought it was that fellow in the basement. Dad got up and went down there and he was sound asleep; he slept good. Many times Dad took people in like that and today we don't do it. We can't trust them today.

Margaret Butler, 87, Steuben County

CHURCH

We went to church every Sunday. That was one thing we always did. It wasn't whether you wanted to go—it was the rule. We never asked. We knew that was part of our routine.

Sunday morning everybody got ready for church. Saturday night was bath night and everybody had to see if they had a pair of stockings to put on clean Sunday morning. If they needed mending, they had to mend their own.

Margaret Butler, 87, Steuben County

Well, going to church was simply one of those things we always did—going to Sunday School and to church. At that time there were no snow plows and I recall going to church in the evening—they would lay down the rail fences on other people's farms—nobody objected— and just simply drive around the snow banks in a bob sled.

I have such a vivid picture of my father standing in the box of the bob sled and hanging on, leaning back to hang onto some horses that were quite frisky.

My mother always heated the soapstone, and there was straw in the box and we sat on blocks of wood and snuggled together and kept warm; but that's the way we went to church in the evening.

Ruth Hostetler, 79, Lagrange County

We went to a little church about a mile and a half from where we lived. Lots of times we walked. Because all the kids down the road walked, so we'd all walk together. Get ready in all (chuckle) your finery—your one nice dress—and walk to church.

Dorothy Hoffman, 59, Adams County

We went to church regularly. I remember in the summertime carry- ing our shoes until we got in sight of the church and then put them on. Shoes were hard to come by back then and we had to conserve them as best we could. That was common practice back then.

Nellie Frakes, 71, Perry County

Of course the men sat on one side of the church, and the women on the other. They had an Amen corner on the women's side and an Amen corner on the men's side. I never heard any Amens scarcely from the women's side.

Mostly the men.

Yes, there would be loud Amens over there.

Pearl McCall, 89, Daviess County

They used to have two stoves. One stove on the men's side and further back the one on the ladies' side, and a long pipe to where the pastor was preaching in the pulpit. The children sat under the pipe and it got awful hot on the head.

Hilda Thomas, 83, Jackson County

I went to the Albright Evangelical Church near Atlanta. It was a one-room building with two coal stoves, one on either side. There would be short seats where the stove stood, and then behind them would be a long seat. This stove would be heated up real hot.

We liked to sit on the long bench behind the stove, because George Julius always sat on the south end of that seat and he chewed tobacco. He'd sit there with his cud of tobacco in his mouth, and ever so often he'd spit and hit a knothole in the floor. Never saw him miss in my life. We teens, we loved to sit there and watch George Julius, and we kept watching for him to miss, but he never did.

Beulah Grinstead, 68, Hamilton County

Our preacher's name was James Maynard. He drove a white horse and buggy many miles to get to our church. He received $6.00 every Sunday. He preached long and loud.

Violet David, 79, Brown County

In 1905 we moved back to Indiana. There were several families living at the location and there were several children. My parents, being devout Christians, my father soon organized a Sunday School and they met each Sunday in the schoolhouse. Later a church was built.

My parents' chief joy was attending church. They never missed and they expected their children to be there also.

Colista Rogers, 88, Pike County

There wasn't any chuch around where we lived, but we had a neighbor and they had Sunday School in their front yard in the afternoon in the summertime. In the wintertime they would have Sunday School at the schoolhouse. But we would always look forward to going to the Sunday School in the afternoon over at Ed Sheeks. In the summertime, they'd have a big bucket of apples they passed out, or some kind of treat, and it was kind of nice.

The kids from all around the county, they would come. He would give the Sunday School lesson, or sometimes she would. They were both good teachers, and so those were happy times.

Mary Sheeks, 73, Lawrence County

At Bethany they only had church services once a month, when the minister came. They would have an all-day meeting then. They would have Sunday School three Sundays a month, but on church day everybody went and that would be a basket dinner.

Juanita Hunter, 81, Scott County

Being in a small church we only had about six or seven people in a Sunday School class. They became your very dear friends. You grew up together, and you shared common interests. In a small church everyone has an opportunity to do something that they're really interested in—to play the piano, to lead songs, to take up the offering, to plan a Christmas gathering. In a small church you can help with everything, because they really do need your help.

I can remember taking real pride in perfect attendance. You'd

A baptism in running water,
as many believed was essential.
Submitted by Orange County

receive a special pin and then you'd add bars each year, and I can remember really taking pride in that.

Judi Merkel, 34, Adams County

I was Lutheran and when I got a little older I had confirmation [classes] on Saturday. In the summertime we used to have what we called "Swede" school. We had to learn Swedish in the summertime and have it in our church work. We had to know the little catechism in Swedish, every bit of it.

Isabella Johnson, 84, Marshall County

The church I went to was the German Reformed Church, and in the morning the preacher preached a German sermon and in the evening

he preached an English sermon. I attended both.
Anna Surfus, 85, DeKalb County

There was German in that church way up in the 20's. They just
wouldn't give it up. Some of the old men were the only ones that
voted, and they just left the German in there.
Thelma Roehr, 69, Posey County

Carmel was a Quaker community. My father came home from service [WWI], and he had no clothes other than his uniform to wear. My
grandfather was so proud of him and he took him to church, but he
was asked to leave, because he had been bearing arms.
Jean Brechbill, 65, DeKalb County

At the church was our community activity outside of school, because
the schools didn't have all the sports that they have nowadays.
At church we had our Sunday School classes and young people on
Sunday evening had B.Y., as we called it. The girls had the Guild Girls
which was the young girl's missionary society. Then, at one time, we
even all got involved with the L.T.L., the youth division of the
W.C.T.U.
We were very busy at church, in fact we were having a Guild vesper
service on December 7, the day the Japanese attacked Pearl Harbor.
That was one of the most solemn vesper services I think that we ever
had in our church.
Betty Alvey, 60, Howard County

The church would put on plays in the wintertime. That would take a
lot of practice, and we all had a lot of fun doing that. We would go
somewhere else to put on this play. Sometimes we'd charge admission
and makes a little money for our group at the church.
In the summertime we had ice cream socials to make money at the
church. We always had one the night before the Fourth of July.
Edna Vandenbark, 92, Vanderburgh County

We had an ice cream social in the summertime. That would always
last two nights. The first night there'd be a whole lot of customers come
out from Washington. The store keepers would come and bring their
whole gang of clerks and delivery boys.
That was the way we helped finance our church. We'd put things in
the church, like a new carpet and new lamps.
Pearl McCall, 89, Daviess County

My parents' lives centered around the church. Their entertainment might consist of singing school at the church. People walked there at night, with their lanterns casting long shadows on the road.

The singing master would have a chart of shaped notes, and he would sing them and the people would sing after him, the different notes and the different melodies. There is where I learned the scale and how to read the shaped notes. They sang everything from church hymns to "Seeing Nellie Home."

Mary Graver, 80, Wayne County

We always had different activities at the church. In the summertime when we had the Children's Day program, that was one of the highlights of the summer. We always had a program at the church at Christmas. We always had a Christmas tree at the church, and we always had the children's program along with it. Then [we had] very significant programs at Easter. And every so often we used to have revival meetings. They used to last, maybe, two weeks.

Bernice Hirst, 87, Lagrange County

The big thing when I was a kid going to church was their Children's Day programs. About two or three times a week all the kids in the neighborhood walked in to practice, and then on Children's Day Sunday we'd put on a program for the parents. That was when our little church was usually full.

Dorothy Hoffman, 59, Adams County

We would have to memorize verses. We all had pieces to say, and I remember my mother making us wreaths of myrtle and white daises. We would have white dresses and had to recite our pieces.

Frances Harley, 89, Marshall County

I remember once when I was a little girl, we had a Children's Day program. I was supposed to sing a simple song, and I proceeded to forget the words. That was the same year that my sister was the little lost sheep. She looked down into the mirror that was supposed to be water, and said right out loud, "Mommy, this isn't water—it's a mirror." The audience really howled at her. She was about three years old.

Mary Ann Moore, 57, Hendricks County

We always had a Christmas program at the church and they'd trim a tree. They had popcorn popped and that was given to the children. And then, when I was in my teens, stick candy was the treat at the churches. They'd have peppermint candy, and lemon drops, and stick candy.

Eldo Bell, 86, Spencer County

My mother said she always dreaded to see Christmas time come, because we had to learn our speeches and the little plays that we were in, and everyone was talking out loud. We were studying, saying our poems, some were reading, and she said that nearly drove her up a wall.

I can imagine trying to help fifteen kids learn their parts, and listening to all that.

Mary Sheeks, 73, Lawrence County

Yes, I remember Christmas—must not forget Christmas. The children always learned pieces at home and then they would have to recite them in front of the congregation and the people were always there in the evening service. Each child had a piece to speak. There were certain ones that would get together and we would sing. I remember one night especially, we had a Christmas tree that almost touched the ceiling in the church. In those days we didn't have electric lights, we had candles and each candle had a holder with a clip on it which would fasten to the limb of the branch of the evergreen tree. There would be lights all over it. The men would come in, and the children would help trim the tree. We'd have tinsel, string popcorn, we didn't have fancy tinsel like they do today. We'd have popcorn that was strung to make the white streamers, there was always one man in the church though, there was always dangers of fire. Cedars will burn very readily, this man was asked to watch the tree so if a candle would light a little branch it would soon be outen. He carried a long fish pole and had a wet rag on the end of that fish pole so that he could reach clear to the top of the tree in case there was a fire and could outen the flame. It was always fun to watch him. You were distracted. You couldn't always keep your mind, as a kid, on what was going on up front.

Alma Knecht, 78, Wabash County

Opal: Another highlight was the camp meeting. We all went to that.

Juanita: It was a social event, but it was a religious camp meeting. Many people rented cabins and then the children would get to go and stay with their friends for a night or two, and that was a wonderful thing.

Opal: Camp meetings would last two weeks and they would have ministers from everywhere. There was just about as good of sermons as you ever heard. But back at that time we were more to have a little fun than we were to go to church. We'd go up there and parade around.

Juanita: That was one time you got to wear your nice dress, if you had one.

Opal Whitsett, 84, and Juanita Hunter, 81, Scott County

When I gave my heart to Christ, there was a protracted meeting, as they used to call it. There was a minister and a song leader who came to the church.

There were 34 people united with the church at that time. My sister older than me was baptized at Nyona Lake. They went across the bridge and up the hill to Smith's to change their clothes. After they were baptized, they wrapped a blanket around them.

Lois Wagoner, 76, Fulton County

At the age of nine I was in an evangelistic meeeting. I mean to tell you, they preached then. I mean to tell you, they really got themselves into it. He got onto the subject of hell. It sounded like a terrible place to me, and I got scared. So I was genuinely born again that night and I've never doubted my salvation since. If I had to be scared into heaven, I'd rather be scared into it than to miss it, wouldn't you?

Then that summer they decided that all the new converts should be baptized. They didn't have baptismals like they do today. No!! It had to be done in a running stream, so I was taken out to a running stream with a group of others who were to be baptized. They had an awful time getting my head under. I didn't want my head under that water.

Beulah Grinstead, 68, Hamilton County

Religion was the thing that stood out in our home. We always had prayers before meals. I never knew of us to sit down to a meal that my father didn't return thanks. Those are the things that stay with you all your life, and you can't get away from it.

Margaret Butler, 87, Steuben County

Our family had family worship night and morning. I learned a lot of Bible. A lot of times, we kids would cut up, and you wouldn't think we'd heard a thing. But we did, and a lot of it stuck.

What was family worship like?

My mother and my dad, they would take turns. They would read the Bible to us and then we knelt down and everybody prayed on their knees.

One night, I never will forget. In the fall, the mice would come in, so a little mouse was playing around. My brother was the only one behaving. All the rest of us were watching the mouse. Well, the mouse ran up the leg of his pants and he went BAM!! and he had him. I never will forget it, because all the rest of us almost burst out laughing, but Mother would have spanked us good if we had.

Beulah Grinstead, 68, Hamilton County

I can remember, as a kid, I wanted to rake up some leaves on Sunday afternoon, just to play in them. But it was "No way!" Dad said, "You are not getting the rake out. We don't do that on Sunday. We honor the Sabbath Day."

Bernice Esch, 70, Lagrange County

My first experience with prayer—with real prayer, not just saying a prayer, but really, really praying for something—was for my Uncle Charles. He was 19 years old and he got peritonitis and he was terribly, terribly sick. He had always lived with us and he was always like my big brother.

I thought he was going to die. I went out in the hay mow and kneeled down out there and prayed for God to cure him. I might have been seven. And he lived.

Pearl Hiland, 96, Fulton County

I became a Christian at age 15, so I had the Holy Spirit's guidance through the most difficult times in one's life, when you make choices of whether you will go to school; what kind of career you will take up; who your friend shall be; who you will marry; you have help in making all these decisions.

I appreciate the fact that I did have this early experience and was able to direct my life a little less willfully and a little more intelligently than I might have done, had I not become a Christian at an early age.

Blanche Burnett, 77, Morgan County

I entered the church at a very early age. I was only nine years old and I always enjoyed the church activities very much. I went to a great many things that the church did, and I went to Sunday School every Sunday. And that's where I got my love for the church, in my early days. And now I have the longest continued membership of anybody in our church, out of 700 people.

Camille Hey, 89, Shelby County

I told my parents this a short time ago. I feel that the religious background that they gave us in my home was more valuable than just about anything else they could have given us.

Mary Helms, 45, Franklin County

He [preacher] and four or five families would go home with us for Sunday dinner.

The women would prepare the dinner. We always baked on Saturdays and dressed the chickens for Sunday. The older people ate first, while all we children waited until they were through, then we ate what was left.

Violet David, 79, Brown County

A Sunday School picnic held in 1908 "at [the] Cave." A sign in the background advertises rental swim suits for 5¢ each.
Submitted by Decatur County

We'd always have a lot of company after church on Sunday. The folks would decide at church and ask somebody home with them after church. And, of course, we were asked to their home for dinner in return sometimes. But I know we, during the fried chicken season, would come home from church and my mother'd go and pick up a chicken, wring its head off, and get it ready, and fry it for dinner. And my sister and I'd go over to the strawberry patch and pick strawberries, and stem them and get them ready for our dessert. And of course, Mother had baked a lot of bread on Saturday, so we had plenty of bread, and sometimes we had plenty of pies. But, in strawberry season we expected to eat strawberries for dessert.

And a lot of our company was relatives because the community was filled with relatives. But not always. When we went to church, there'd be the church members, not relatives at all, that would come home with us. And then in return we'd go to their houses sometimes. Sort of take turns doing that.

Lennie Hern, 90, Decatur County

After church, we would go to someone's home for dinner. There were a number of families that rotated. We'd have dinner, then stay and play all afternoon, have supper and go to prayer meeting that night.

We kids looked forward to that in the summer. In the winter, we'd see each other at school, but in summertime we could hardly wait for Sunday to all get together again.

Nellie Frakes, 71, Perry County

On Sundays everybody got together. We would go to church and then somebody would say, "Oh, come go home with us," or they would go home with us. Maybe if they had something special for dinner, they'd go home and get it and bring it.

All the young people came to our house on Sunday. We had a great big yard where we'd play party games, and Mother would make homemade ice cream. Just about every Sunday they would come.

And then, my brother-in-law's mother, they would go to their house, because they would have several young people, and she would cook a great big kettle of either beans or cornbread; or, in the summertime, green beans and corn. Everyone would just go in and enjoy it.

We had lots of fun. It wasn't anything like the entertainment they have today, but at the party games maybe there would be 50 young people would come to our home, because we had a larger home and there were more young people there.

Elma Matthew, 74, Madison County

Did you have a church group?

We did have what we called Epworth League, and we had a get-together Sunday nights after church. We called it the Popcorn club. We had a lot of fun. Most of us sang in the choir—we had a nice choir. One family had a lot of boys, and a lot of these boys went with the different girls. We had fun—clean fun!!

Did you know from one Sunday to the next who was going to entertain?

We may have. Anyway, there was always a place to go.

You mentioned pulling taffy. Who prepared the taffy for you?

I suppose the mother in whichever home we were in. I remember one
girl's mother made us fudge. She made the best fudge—I can taste it
yet—big thick creamy fudge. Of course, we had to have popcorn, for
we called it the Popcorn Club.

Lora Herrick, 89, Cass County

FUNERALS

Funerals are handled so differently now. I remember before they did
any embalming and kept the body in the home. The neighbors would
wash and dress the body and place it on a cooling board until rigor
mortis set in. The body was placed in the casket and the casket put in
the parlor, or a room that wasn't used much.

The body wasn't kept very long, especially in hot weather. Then
gradually they began to embalm. At first the undertaker would come
to the home and do the embalming there; then they began taking the
body to the funeral home to embalm it and then returned it to the
home.

The funeral was always held at the church.

When the body was kept at home, there was always someone, or
maybe several, who would sit up all night with the body. They would
have coffee and lunch at midnight. It was almost like a picnic,
sometimes.

I well remember the first one I knew of where they didn't stay all
night with the corpse. It was a neighbor of ours. Her son was a profes-
sor from the city and about 10 o'clock he asked them all to leave, so
the family could get some rest. I never will forget the reaction. They
felt it was almost blasphemy because he didn't want someone to stay
with the body. Customs really do change.

Nellie Frakes, 71, Perry County

Two people or more would set up with the corpse at night. I suppose
that came from the time when the houses were open, with no screens,
and the body had to be protected. But then it just became a tradition.
People did that until they began to use funeral homes for the corpse.

They always went and set up. People would take in cake and cookies and pie.

Beulah Mardis, 76, Johnson County

Juanita: My mother always went whenever there was a death in the family, and she did the sewing. She would ride horseback and she put me on the back of her side saddle. She would go to the home and make the shroud for the child or lady who had passed away.

If it happened on her bread baking day, she would take a basket on her arm and take her bread [dough] along and bake it while we were there.

Opal: You'd always sit up with the corpse. There was a certain group in the county that usually did that—Zelma and Bourke Blocher and Homer and I—we'd say, "Don't worry, we'll be there." I could go up and down the road and name you the ones that lived there and that we have sat up with.

When I was a girl at home, Mother always did like Juanita's mother. She always went and helped lay out the corpse. There was a little girl who got burned awful bad one time, and Mother went to lay her out and she didn't have a helper, so I was the helper.

That was the last time I ever went with her when she was going to do that. I was just a kid, and that was enough of that. I didn't want to do it any more.

Juanita: I remember my first experience. I had gone horseback when Noble Sipes' little baby had passed away and I had sat up all night. The undertaker from Crothersville came and asked me if I would help dress the baby. I said, "Oh, no," but he said I wouldn't have to touch him, and I had sat up all night keeping moisture on his eyelids anyway. So he went in the room and picked him up and put the little dress on him and said, "Now you button the dress." My hand slipped and that was my first experience touching a dead person. I could do anything to anyone after that, because the fear was gone.

Opal Whitsett, 84, and Juanita Hunter, 81, Scott County

When I was a child and there was a funeral, people would go in and help. If there was washing to be done, my mother would bring the washing and ironing home. If there were children in the family, they would take care of the children. The neighbors would go in and clean the house and they would bring food.

Virlee Jochum, 64, Dubois County

There would always be some of the closest neighbors that would go and just stay at the home and get the meals and other neighbors brought the food in. Really, you were never alone. There was somebody there all the time. The body was kept at home and people just came to call and were in and out all the time. There was somebody there all the time.

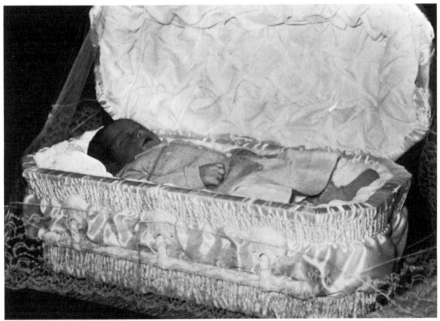

Families who had not had photographs made previously often took pictures of dead babies so that they could have something to remember of their short lives.
Submitted by Newton County

Did they put a wreath on the door?

Yes, and if they were a business person, there was a wreath on the door at the store in town.

Helen Musselman, 66, Hamilton County

In my day they used to hang crepe on the door when somebody died. Yes, and the clocks were stopped and the window shades were drawn down.

Ellen McAfee, 69, Marshall County

They used to have funerals in the home. It was kind of bad, because you would always look in that corner of the room and think about it

and that was sad. When my brother-in-law was buried, the funeral was
in the house and his mother could hardly go in that front room for a
long, long time.

Margaret Gibson, 87, Cass County

They didn't take care of them like they do now. I remember one funeral where they had somebody sit and use a fan to keep the flies away.
They didn't always embalm them then. And I remember at Aunt Julie's
funeral they had her in the home, and they had a pole at the end of the
casket with drapes all around it to keep the flies out.

Grace Elrod, 85, Jasper County

I remember my mother, if somebody died, going out in the garden
and getting snowballs and poppies and different kinds of flowers and
make them into a little bundle [bouquet] and take them over to the
neighbors for the funeral. And there they'd be, at the head of the coffin. Now people wouldn't think of doing that, but there was love in it.

Alvah Watson, 97, Allen County

The body was embalmed and brought in the home and the casket
was in the home and the funeral was in the home. In our community
they didn't even take them to the church for the funeral. There were
floral bouquets, a lot of them were homemade, and some were bought.

They had flower girls. After the service was over, the girls lined up in
two rows and they would give each one of them a bouquet or basket of
flowers. Then the pallbearers would carry the corpse out through this
aisle to the hearse. And, I hate to say it, that was a big day for us, for
we always got to dress up in our finest and be flower girls.

Opal Gallagher, 72, Shelby County

Everyone went to funerals in those days. The church bell would toll
out the person's age; pause; then toll out the hour of the funeral. We
would stop working and get ready and go. Some times it was a friend
and sometimes a total stranger.

Violet David, 79, Brown County

The undertaker came back with the hearse, drawn by horses. The
dead person was taken to the church, where a long personal sermon
about his life was preached. Then he was buried in the nearby
graveyard.

When I was about twelve years old, my sister and I were pallbearers
for a little girl. She was a small girl and that was quite a tragedy and I
really grieved for that little girl.

Margaret Garrison, 82, Wabash County

As we'd go through town, we'd hear the bell toll. I can still hear the toll of the bell as we drove in the funeral procession. It was horses and buggies, so it was quiet and you could hear.

Alvah Watson, 97, Allen County

They had hearses with black horses and they had to walk. They couldn't trot or drive fast; they had to walk. When they got almost to the gate to go into the cemetery, the undertaker and all of the men would take off their hats.

Margaret Garrison, 82, Wabash County

After church Sunday dinner was served on white linen and using good china. Friends often shared this meal.
Submitted by an Extension Homemaker

Your neighbors and friends dug the grave. They were usually buried in a church cemetery. You didn't have your big cemeteries like they do now. They were buried in a small church cemetery where the friends and neighbors had dug the grave, and where they re-covered it afterwards.

Edna Klinstiver, 58, Floyd County

Our folks had a cemetery lot. I remember one time my father took my older brother and me and we got the gravel bed and we went down along the highway and he would have us cut some sod, little bunches, and lay it in the wagon. We took that down to our cemetery lots. My brother and I would tramp, tramp, tramp and we hauled water from the creek a short distance away. We sodded that lot and it's still sodded—I suppose the same sod.

My father died in 1923 and in 1924 my mother said, "I would like to take some peonies out to the cemetery." My father and my youngest sister were already dead and there was a place for Mother. We went out and dug a red peony and a pink peony and a white one. We took them down there and Mother said, "We'll give Bertha the pink one and we'll give Daddy the red one and I'll take the white one." We had to take water and set them out. I remember so well.

And they're still there! My niece was here last week and she had been to the cemetery and she said it was a beautiful sight. This Decoration Day they were all out in bloom. And that was in 1924.

Alvah Watson, 97, Allen County

ENTERTAINMENT

We lived in the same neighborhood as my grandparents and our father and mother. Both were from big families, so we had lots of cousins that we grew up with. At that time people stayed where they were born more than they do now. They didn't go moving like they do today. We grew up with our cousins, and I think back on the good times we had.

We had a happy childhood and a happy young life. It was altogether different than what it is today, because we didn't get very far from home. The church and the school were the social contacts at the time we were growing up. We weren't entertained like the young people are today. We played our own games.

We played together and were always at someone's house. The whole gang was there. All the young people in the neighborhood would come. Sunday afternoons, that was our special time to play together. We'd be first one house on Sunday afternoons, then somebody's else's house the next Sunday. We'd meet and jump the rope and play hide and seek and drop the handkerchief and all those things, until we grew older and outgrew those things. But until we got to high school, that was what we entertained ourselves doing.

And there would be neighborhood parties and that would be from one home to another and that would be through the week.

And the things that went on at the schoolhouse and the church was our social life. That was where we had our spelling bees and fun things, at the schoolhouse and the church.

Zelma Blocher, 81, Scott County

We'd go as groups and almost always be invited and end up in someone's home, where they'd serve something very meager. Apples, popcorn, something homegrown because they didn't have money to spend. No one expected to be entertained with anything that cost money.

Virgie Bowers, 81, Pulaski County

Did you have parties then?
Oh, yes, lots of parties. We weren't supposed to dance, but we did. We called them party games, but now they call them round or barn dances. Well, not so much—we would just sing and whirl and dance around. There was no pattern to it.

Then we had taffy pullings, popped corn and all kind of get-togethers. I had a nice home to entertain in, and willing parents that could do it.

Pearl Hiland, 96, Fulton County

I had six sisters and two brothers.
What did you do for fun?
We had church socials and class socials in the schools. Our family was always ready to open up the home for a party, because parties were always in the home. It used to be kind of comical, because by the time you got a bunch of young people active in the home, something usually got broken. If it wasn't the glass out of the door, it might have been the end of what we called a divan.

And my father always said we had parties every change of the moon. We had church parties and school parties and there was several of us. It did seem kind of often. But Mother always said she'd rather we would have the party at home and then she knew where we were at and what we were doing.

Beulah Rawlings, 76, Hamilton County

I think I remember the gatherings at our home about as much as anything, because Mother was very good about wanting us to be at home with our friends. So we had taffy-pulling parties and we played card games by the hour and we had our group which just gathered at our house most of the time.

We spent more time at home than anything else because the children were welcome there even up into our teenage years. She always welcomed our friends and so we felt very much at home there, and I think our friends did, too. She made doughnuts for us and things like that.

And I had a very, very happy childhood and I remember it that way.

Mary Helms, 45, Franklin County

One of the biggest things when I was growing up was Chautauqua. These different entertainers and speakers from all over the world came, and that was a wonderful thing. They set this big tent up on the fairgrounds, and that tent was filled up every night. It lasted for a week.

Then, of course, there was the county fair. That was a big thing.

Did they have judges for different days for different livestock?

Yes, and then we had horse races at the county fair. We had a little race horse and my mother would race him. There was no money, no betting. I expect our county fair was as big as any county had. There were entries in canning and dressmaking and other home economics projects. And the farmers showed their grains.

Another big thing in the winter was the Farmers Institute. That was sponsored by Purdue. The Farmers Institute was a big thing. It lasted a week. [It was held] at Liberty in the courthouse and that big courtroom would be full. We had speakers from Purdue.

And the county fair, the Chautauqua, the Farmers Institute and our church activities, and that was just about it.

Gleda Stevens, Union County

There's one thing I'd like to tell that we had in the summer. We had Chautauqua that would come. They would hold it under a big tent and speakers from way off would come and speak. That was one of the highlights of the summer. That would have been about 1908 and 1909.

What did they talk about?

Well, they would put on religious plays and they would give lectures and bring the outside world to us. Things that we didn't have any way of hearing about.

How long would they be there?

About two weeks. We tried to go every night, because we felt that it was education and we learned so much.

Juanita Hunter, 81, Scott County

We had Chautauqua right out there in Beechwood Park for years. It came from Chautauqua Lake in New York. They had an organization there to plan the Chautauquas that went all over the United States. And they were big—we even had President Taft come one time. They said there were 5,000 people in Beechwood Park that day.

They had tents all over the place. The farmers would come in and that was their vacation. They had a nice restaurant tent in there, or you could do your own cooking. Lots took their tents and tented out for ten days. The farmers would go home of a morning and evening to do their chores and then come back.

They had all kinds of the best music and talent. They had a place where they took care of the littlest children. There was little beds for them and they had someone to take care of them during the program.

And if it had been a very dry summer, we could be sure it would rain during Chautauqua. We did just about every year—we had a storm and a good rain during Chautauqua. It was pretty exciting in those tents. Sometimes you would get wet, even though you were inside.

Hazel Thomas, 81, Parke County

At Chautauqua was the first time I ever saw mediums make horns float through the air, and weird things like that. They really put on a show with jugglers and all sort of things.

Beulah Grinstead, 68, Hamilton County

I remember the street fair. They had a dog and pony show. I even remember the ponies' names yet: Keeno and Goldie. The little dogs would jump on the horses' backs. Goldie was a little yellow pony and Keeno was spotted.

Eunice Houze, 75, Ohio County

As far as I know, I never missed a [county] fair after I was old enough to go. The first fairs I remember, we went in a carriage. We forded the river on the east side of the fairgrounds. We always took our dinner with us and then we would have a picnic, not only with our family, but with other families of our friends and neighbors. Going to the fair was one of the highlights of our summer.

Another thing I enjoyed was the balloon ascension. I always wanted to watch the balloon go up, and that was a great thing. We'd sit on the hillside and watch that balloon being filled with gas. Just to watch it when it was cut loose and drift across the river. It was always interesting to know where it was going to come down.

Harriet Gwinnup, 73, Fayette County

I've always been a State Fair lover. Always gone to the State Fair since I can remember.

We used to get up long before daylight and Mother would pack our lunch. We always had fried chicken and cake and pie and bean salad or potato salad. We packed it in a nickel basket, as we called it then, with a cloth over the top.

We started driving the horses to the Fair and we started early in the morning. To this day, when I'm going to the State Fair, I feel I should get up early like that. One time I did get down there before the buildings opened.

When our kids were in 4-H we were still taking our dinners and spreading out on the grass and eating. All of us folks from Union Township that had 4-H youngsters went. I had some pictures of us all sitting around on the ground eating. Today you would be afraid to eat that food, but we never had any bad results.

Thelma Dye, 83, Boone County

CIRCUS

I remember one time in the afternoon about 3 o'clock, a man come up our driveway on a horse—a beautiful horse and had a shiny bridle. The saddle was beautiful. And the man had a long mustache that was curled out. It looked like handlebars on a bicycle.

He said he was a roustabout for the circus—a wagon circus that traveled from place to place by road. He said the circus was coming and he wanted to see if they could use our school ground for a stopping place, to feed the animals and have a rest.

So they made all the arrangements for the circus to come and spend the day there.

Well, you know, our boys scattered out and they passed the word around to all the people. And you never saw as many people looking through the crack in the fence as we did when that circus came.

It was a beautiful thing. Wagons with beautiful painting, color on the side and animals in there. They had two elephants and a couple of camels—oh, it was exciting. But they didn't have to tell us to stay on the other side of the fence, because we were all afraid, because we never saw a lion before.

But that was outstanding! To see those wagons coming and then to see it leaving. We didn't miss one thing. I suppose that was one of the nicest things we kids ever had. I never saw so many kids in my life. We would line up along the fence and we'd look through the cracks in the fence and we'd watch everything.

Scene on the midway of the
Indiana State Fair.
J. C. Allen Collection

You had your own personal circus?
Yes, and it was wonderful.
Alvah Watson, 97, Allen County

MOVIES

Did they have a movie at Kewanna?

They never had a movie until, it must have been about 1918 or 1919.
They called it a nickelodeon. It only cost a nickel.

Pearl Hiland, 96, Fulton County

We lived just south of Bass Lake about a mile and a half. And our
one big outing in the summer all through my younger years was this:
we would go up to and around the lake to a little corner called Wy-
nona. And we went to the movies—just once in the summer. Hitched
up a team and rode the wagon to go to the movies.

And this was with your family?

Yes, as a family. Oh, no, you didn't go otherwise. You went as a
family. And we got to go that one night. That was our summer
recreation.

Edna Winter, 74, Pulaski County

When did you attend your first movie? Do you remember that?

I am not sure it was the first, but this is the one that impressed me
the most. Melvin and I came into Rochester, at the Paramount
Theater on the west side of Main Street.

And it [the show] was "Where is My Wandering Boy Tonight?" I'll
never forget it; everybody in the house was crying before it was over.

Was it a silent movie?

Must have been. There was music, but, yes, I think the story was
printed.

Somebody probably played the piano.

Yes.

Lois Wagoner, 76, Fulton County

Then later on they put on the movies that you could listen to and see
pictures at the same time, and we went to those. My husband enjoyed
them very much.

Mildred Cochran, Switzerland County

The first moving picture show that I saw, we got there late. My
brother and I were interested in it. There was one place where a gypsy
was stabbed, so when the show was over, everybody walked out and
we did, too.

The woman at the desk said we should go back and see the first part
of it. Well, we watched and watched, and when the time came that man

was going to get stabbed, I hid my eyes. I didn't want to watch it.

Grace Heinzman, 86, Hamilton County

You mentioned free shows. Were they in town?

Well, we had them at Oxford and Otterbein. Both were in the town square. A man would come and set up his outfit, and we all sat on the ground. Or, if you brought chairs, [you would] sit in chairs and watch free shows.

Do you remember some of the titles of the shows?

We thought more of cartoons than anything else. They were mainly like the things you see now [when you have] re-runs of early shows. They were silent, you had to be able to read to be able to get the meaning of it.

Pearl Sollars, 70, Tippecanoe County

Now on Saturday nights we went to town; we went to the free shows in Reynolds. We went to buy our groceries, and that was your one big night out, on Saturday night.

What were free movies?

Well, in a little area off of the main street in Reynolds there was seats, some of them were just boards set on blocks. They were just like benches you would find out in a park. And they were lined up so many people could set and see the screen.

And they had a little building about the size of an outhouse that the projector was in. I am not sure how long the movies ran—I am sure half an hour or forty-five minutes. It wasn't a long, lengthy thing.

You didn't pay, you just went and sat. Some towns used to have them twice a week, you could go on Wednesday nights and Saturday nights, but I just remember Saturday nights.

I remember Abbott and Costello, Charlie Chaplin, and the cartoons with the cat and Mickey Mouse. Do you remember the train?

Oh, yes, sometimes they shut the movie off and waited until it went through. Or sometimes you just sat through it. It was a steam engine and very noisy. It just rocked you where you were sitting, because that's where the show was, right along the railroad track there.

Alene McKinley, 47, White County

On Saturday afternoon, when Daddy worked in town, we girls would stay in town all day and see Gene Autry and all those shows. We only had one car, so we had to go when Daddy went to work.

Was it just a one-time showing?

I'm not real clear. I know if they played it over, you could stay. I don't remember the price, but it was just a little—or we couldn't have afforded it.

Juanita Harden, 49, Bartholomew County

Did you have any heroes or models at this time?
Oh, yes, I admired Douglas Fairbanks and really was charmed by Mary Pickford.

Gladys Tribolet, 70, Huntington County

Do you remember Deanna Durbin? I thought she was so beautiful. I always enjoyed her pictures.

Juanita Harden, 49, Bartholomew County

I just wondered if you had a favorite movie star?
We didn't see too many movies. I read about quite a few of them in the paper. I guess Gene Autry and Roy Rogers and them. We went to see more of that kind of movies than anything.

Edna Klinstiver, 58, Floyd County

Of all the actors and actresses, whom did you think was the best-looking and exciting?
Clark Gable and Betty Grable. I saw Gone With the Wind, which Clark Gable was in, and then I saw it on TV.

Wanda Couch, 48, Clark County

My mother said the big thing was, every Saturday night you [would] load up the kids and go down to Franklin Street which was then a nice place to go and you would go to the movies, and the kids went, too.

She said that they had a crying room, and if you had little kids you sat back there with your husband and watched the show.

Then they would go get an ice cream cone and go home. That was the highlight of the whole week, other than going to church.

Theresa McFadin, 29, Posey County

And it seemed like you never lacked for something to be doing. We had a lot of good times, but we were doing good things. No one seemed to be doing things that they shouldn't be doing. And we just thoroughly enjoyed doing the good things.

Virgie Bowers, 81, Pulaski County

ACKNOWLEDGMENTS

A statewide project done almost completely through volunteer work owes so much to so many people that no list could possibly include the names of all who contributed to its success. The membership of IEHA and the general public have enthusiastically supported and encouraged the project from its inception.

The volunteer interviewers who conducted the fine interviews which are the basis of the whole project spent long undocumented hours, as they conducted the interviews and, in many cases, transcribed them also. Their contribution is incalculable.

Equally vital to the project are the narrators. The people who talked with the interviewers shared with us their experiences, their memories and their values. These detailed and intimate reminiscences form the rich motherlode from which the books are drawn. As they shared their thoughts with us, they helped us document a way of life which is nearly gone now.

The list which concludes this section contains the names of narrator first, interviewer second, listed by county in alphabetical order. Without the peole named in this section, there could have been no project.

Because of space limitations, this book can contain only a very small portion of the fine material contained in the interviews. Every interview has been read and studied many times. All are extremely useful for background and research, both in this project and for future historians.

Many thanks go also to the women who shared their photographs and other visual materials with us. Their contributions were vital to the project, adding a very important dimension.

Chief consultant to the project from the beginning has been F. Gerald Handfield. The project owes much of its depth and scope in the initial planning and implementation to his oral history knowledge and to his interest and enthusiasm.

Paul Wilson, photographer and producer, traveled many miles in recording the visual material and continues to give his professional advice. His expertise and unfailing dependability have been much appreciated.

Other consultants who have shared their insights have been D'Ann Campbell, Indiana University; Alice Shrock, Earlham College; and Cullom Davis, Sangamon State University, Illinois.

The Oral History Committee of the IEHA has given advice, inspiration and hard work to the project. They have indexed interviews and sorted excerpts to make a large body of information more accessible. They have traveled many miles and manned many sales booths at IEHA functions and the Indiana State Fair. Current members are Coleen Allmandinger, Betty Alvey, Julia Binkley, Margaret McClain, Jeanette Ponsford, and Nancy Jo Prue. Former members are Dorothy Anderson, Annette Hitch and Bettie MacMorran. Margaret Boilanger has kept perfect financial records for the project and Coleen Allmandinger has coordinated publicity. Betty Alvey has spent many extra hours mailing book orders and slide/tape programs. Julia Binkley has been interviewer-in-chief as she has taped interviews with special people in IEHA's history.

The members of the IEHA Board of Directors have been very supportive as have the cooperative extension home economics agents in all the counties. Ann Hancook, IEHA advisor, has been particularly helpful.

Thanks are due to the Indiana Committee for the Humanities for past financial and moral support; and to the Indiana Historical Society for making its personnel, facilities and files available, and for agreeing to serve as final repository for original materials from the project.

Purdue University, Indiana University, and Indiana State Library have served as cooperating institutions, sharing their personnel and facilities.

A final word of deep appreciation goes to all the members of my family who have been so interested and supportive throughout the project. Our family has had two marriages, a law school graduation, and three grandchildren born during the course of the project, amply demonstrating that we are all homemakers together. And, like our narrators, my deepest thanks and affection go to my husband who has supported me fully and given me all his encouragement at the times that mattered most.

LIST OF SOURCES

INTERVIEWEE, *INTERVIEWER*

ADAMS COUNTY
Dorothy Hoffman, *Brenda Else*
Donna Marbach, *Brenda Else*
Judi Merkel, *Brenda Else*
Esther Striker, *Brenda Else*
Sarah Zeigler, *Brenda Else*

ALLEN COUNTY
Agnes Emenhiser, *Glendora Gruelach*
Hope Kessler, *Glendora Gruelach*
Alvah Watson, *Glendora Gruelach*
Mary Yerks, *Glendora Gruelach*

BARTHOLOMEW COUNTY
Juanita Harden, *Joyce Meier*
Libby McKinley, *Veda Eddy*
Patricia Ritchey, *Joyce Meier*
Ruth Thompson, *Julia Binkley*

BENTON COUNTY
Hazel Clawson, *Achsa Nussbaum*
Bertha Pampel, *Achsa Nussbaum*
Wilma Potter, *Nancy Prue*

BLACKFORD COUNTY
Mary Shields, *Margaret Keller*
Betty Trout, *Jan Barger*
Mable Wingate, *Margaret Keller*

BOONE COUNTY
Thelma Dye, *Mildred Collins*
Wilbur Whitehead, *Mildred Collins*
Martha Whitehead, *Mildred Collins*
Shirley Woody, *Julia Binkley*

BROWN COUNTY
Violet David, *Garnet Parsley*
Dorothy Dine, *Garnet Parsley*
Iva Kelp, *Garnet Parsley*
Garnet Parsley, *Dorothy Dine*
Murriel Sisson, *Shirley Campbell*

CARROLL COUNTY
Pearl Garrison, *Betty Smith*

CASS COUNTY
Ilo Coffing, *Margaret McClain*
Margaret Gibson, *Margaret McClain*
Lora Herrick, *Margaret McClain*
Jean Murphy, *Margaret McClain*

CLARK COUNTY
Wanda Couch, *Carol Haas*
Nina Diefenbach, *Julia Binkley*
Ellen Doss, *Deborah Gleason*

INTERVIEWEE, *INTERVIEWER*

CLAY COUNTY
Gaby Moon, *Anne Harshbarger*

CLINTON COUNTY
Mary Dean, *Marilyn Beard*
Dorothy McGill, *Marilyn Beard*

CRAWFORD COUNTY
The Tower family, *Sharon Broughton*

DAVIESS COUNTY
Doris Chapman, *Ruth Colbert*
Ruth Bateman, *Thelma Bingham*
Jane Gillooly, *Thelma Bingham*
Verona Lemmon, *Ruth Colbert*
Pearl McCall, *Ruth Colbert*

DEARBORN COUNTY
Elizabeth Elbrecht, *Doris Marple &
  Edith Mackey*
JoAnn Folke, *Julia Binkley*
Sarah Whitham, *Edith Mackey*

DECATUR COUNTY
Erma Agnew, *Lorene Shirk*
Lena Alverson, *Lorene Shirk*
Marie Clark, *Lorene Shirk*
Sadie Davis, *Lorene Shirk*
Lennie Hern, *Lorene Shirk*
Irene Redington, *Lorene Shirk*
Lorene Shirk, *Lorene Shirk*

DEKALB COUNTY
Sarah Amstutz, *Ruth Overmyer*
Jean Brechbill, *Maxine Harvey*
Phyllis Frank, *Maxine Harvey*
Hazel Norden, *Maxine Harvey*
Anna Surfus, *Maxine Harvey*

DELAWARE COUNTY
Katherine Bothel, *Uva Ritchie*
Edna Hiatt, *Marjorie Quick*
Rosanna Scott, *Margaret McClain*
Mary Wright, *Uva Ritchie*

DUBOIS COUNTY
Otillia Buehler, *Betty Heichelbech*
Verlee Jochum, *Mary Jo Niehaus &
  Jeanette Raucher*
Rosalia Mehringer, *Mary Jo Niehaus*
Alma Small, *Jeanette Rauscher*
Norma Trent, *Mary Jo Niehaus*

INTERVIEWEE, *INTERVIEWER*

FAYETTE COUNTY
Deanna Barricklow, *Virginia Mason*
Harriet Gwinnup, *Virginia Mason*
Thelma Robeson, *Donna Scott*
Maud Sloneker, *Virginia Mason*
Sharon Windhorst, *Donna Scott*

FLOYD COUNTY
Edna Klinstiver, *Mary O'Bryan*
Mary Flispart, *Mary O'Bryan*
Mary Schoen, *Mary O'Bryan*

FOUNTAIN COUNTY
Lena Foster, *Willa Hoagland &
Laverna Galloway*
Mary George
Nina Gray

FRANKLIN COUNTY
Elsie Bossert, *Maribel Wilson*
Mary Helms, *Maribel Wilson*
Rebecca Stewart, *Maribel Wilson*
Martha Werner, *Myrna Geisting*
Hazel Williams, *Myrna Geisting*

FULTON COUNTY
Trella Feidner, *Doris Hill*
Pearl Hiland, *Shirley Willard*
Irene Rouch, *Doris Hill*
Lois Wagoner, *Shirley Willard*

GIBSON COUNTY
Floy Jacobus, *Ruby Rumble*
Essie Rumble, *Ruby Rumble*
Beatrice Shuel, *Ruby Rumble*

GRANT COUNTY
Berniece Corey, *Zada McMillan*
Mary Foltz, *Lauretta Brock*
Mary Ann Hoskins, *Marjorie
McDonough*
Icil Hughes, *Marjorie McDonough*
Zada McMillan, *Lauretta Brock*
Edna Maddox, *Marjorie McDonough*
Helen Shockey, *Lauretta Brock*
Alberta Trout, *Zada McMillan*
Alma Smith, *Marjorie McDonough*

GREENE COUNTY
Lula Hasler, *Mildred Duzan*
Blanche Heaton, *Olive Wade*
Gloria Huey, *Julia Binkley*
Anna Workman, *Olive Wade*

HAMILTON COUNTY
Agnes Bell, *Wanetta Edgerly*
Alice Gentry, *Naomi Williamson*
Beulah Grinstead, *Wanetta Edgerly*
Grace Heinzman, *Sandra Wire*
Helen Musselman, *Wanetta Edgerly*
Beulah Rawlings, *Sandra Wire*

INTERVIEWEE, *INTERVIEWER*

HANCOCK COUNTY
Helen Rushton, *JoEllyn Kennedy*
Mary Swarts, *Julia Binkley*
Mary White, *Louise Garrett*

HARRISON COUNTY
Leora Haub, *Elaine Crawford*
Maude Faith, *Diana Kirk*
Ola Kintner, *Ruth Rosenbarger*
Sue Cole, *Elaine Crawford*
Catherine Summers, *Elaine Crawford*
Ozetta Sullivan, *Elaine Crawford*

HENDRICKS COUNTY
Flossie Foster, *Dorothy Kelley*
Leona Hunt, *Mary Moore*
Dorothy Kelley, *Mary Moore*
Mary Moore, *Dorothy Kelley*
Mildred Newby, *Mary Moore*

HENRY COUNTY
Dora Mattox, *Cordelia Wright*
Cheryl Moore, *Cordelia Wright*

HOWARD COUNTY
Betty Alvey, *Rose Russell*
Edna Vandenbark, *Betty Closson*

HUNTINGTON COUNTY
Cora Keplinger, *Pat Fitch*
Doris McFadden, *Coleen Allmandinger*
Masa Scheerer, *Mona Harley*
Isabel Schoeff, *Pat Fitch*
Gladys Tribolet, *Mona Harley*
Mary Wolf, *Pat Fitch*

JACKSON COUNTY
Luella Abell, *Margaret McClain*
Susie Burkhart, *Judith Wichman*
Hilda Thomas, *Judith Wichman*

JASPER COUNTY
Opal Amsler, *Sharon Schulenberg*
Florence DeYong, *Laverne Terpstra*
Grace Elrod, *Rachel Tulera*
Mabel Hunter, *Laverne Terpstra*
Inez Walther, *Laverne Terpstra*

JAY COUNTY
Joan Ford, *Gladys Houser*
Thelma Reedy, *Gladys Houser*
Thelora Shoemaker, *Gladys Houser*
Ruth Shrack, *Gladys Houser*

JENNINGS COUNTY
Ada Clarkson, *Mary Bowman*
Lillian Gookins, *Jacqueline Nentrup*

JOHNSON COUNTY
Elsie Canary, *Carol Spurgeon*
Beulah Mardis, *Carol Spurgeon*

KNOX COUNTY
Hazel Dolkey, *Grace Kocher*
Mara Meyer, *Grace Kocher*
Mona Winkler, *Grace Kocher*

INTERVIEWEE, *INTERVIEWER*

KOSCIUSKO COUNTY
Alice Jones, *Lucy Dockery*
Mary Smoker, *Lucy Dockery*

LAGRANGE COUNTY
Bernice Esch, *Sherrill Vardaman*
Bernice Hirst, *Sherrill Vardaman*
Dora Giggy, *Judy Dintaman*
Ruth Hostetler, *Sherrill Vardaman*

LAKE COUNTY
Nellie Depew, *Eleanor Arnold*

LAPORTE COUNTY
Beverly Barnes, *Marilynn Livinghouse*
Florence Carson, *Marilynn Livinghouse*
Carol Kobat, *Marilynn Livinghouse*
Karren Saboski, *Sherry Deutscher*

LAWRENCE COUNTY
Eula Kelso, *Phyllis Westfall*
Vida Mundy, *Phyllis Westfall*
Mary Sheeks, *Phyllis Westfall*

MADISON COUNTY
Ruth Dane, *Kay Kinnaman*
Loranelle Kimmerling, *Kay Kinnaman*
Elma Matthew, *Judy Smith*
Evelyn Rigsby, *Kay Kinnaman*

MARION COUNTY
Beulah Thompson, *Jerry Handfield*
Sue Zobbe, *Sue Zobbe*

MARSHALL COUNTY
Lulu Graves, *Jean Rectenbaugh*
Lucille Greenlee, *Jean Rectenbaugh*
Isabella Johnson, *Jean Rectenbaugh*
Jean Rectenbaugh, *Jean Rectenbaugh*
Frances Harley, *Lucille Greenlee*
Mary Hawkinson, *Jean Rectenbaugh*
Ada Hutchings, *Jean Rectenbaugh*
Ellen McAfee, *Lucille Greenlee*
Helen Samuelson, *Jean Rectenbaugh*
Ruth Snyder, *Jean Rectenbaugh*

MARTIN COUNTY
Cleo Borders, *Ina Baker*
Ruth Dye, *Ina Baker*
Dorothy Fuhrman, *Carla Hoffman*
Grace Hawkins, *Carla Hoffman*

MIAMI COUNTY
Donna Agness, *Margaret McClain*
Chloe Golden, *Margaret McClain*

MONROE COUNTY
Edith Lawson, *Mabel Mood*
Emily McConnel, *Mabel Mood*
Muriel Voliva, *Mabel Mood*

MORGAN COUNTY
Archie Burnett, *Blanche Burnett*
Blanche Burnett, *Lisa Wilson*
Janice Enk, *Julia Binkley*

INTERVIEWEE, *INTERVIEWER*

MONTGOMERY COUNTY
Frances Bennett, *Janice Harris*
Isabel Cash, *Janice Harris*
Ethel Downen, *Dee Ann Cabell*
Juliana Huseman, *Dee Ann Cabell*

NEWTON COUNTY
Hi Neighbors, *Janet Boston*

NOBLE COUNTY
Della Ackerman, *Jeanette Jacob*
Opal Becker, *Jeanette Jacob*
Joy LeCount, *Coleen Allmandinger*
Dorothy Raub, *Jeanette Jacob*
Lucile Imes, *Jeanette Jacob*
Helen Schinbeckler, *Coleen Allmandinger*

OHIO COUNTY
Clara Ashcraft, *Hazel Sullender*
Eunice Houze, *Hazel Sullender &*
Betty Taylor

OWEN COUNTY
Pearl Kincaid, *Mary Weilhamer*
Jane White, *Mary Weilhamer*

PARKE COUNTY
Stella Irwin, *Ellen Lang*
Hazel Thomas, *Priscilla O'Haver*
Clyde Smith, *Ellen Lang*
Theresa Bramblett, *Priscilla O'Haver*
Myrtle Fisher, *Ellen Lang*
Laura Drake, *Priscilla O'Haver*

PERRY COUNTY
Rosemary Flamion, *Nellie Frakes*
Nellie Frakes, *Nellie Frakes*
Mary Gleeson, *Nellie Frakes*
Florence LaGrange, *Marie Lynch*
Cledia Bertke, *Becky Blum*

PIKE COUNTY
Marjorie Malott, *Marjorie Malott*
Colista Rogers, *Marjorie Malott*

PORTER COUNTY
Margaret Larson
Elsie Nickel
Eulalia Slater, *Claudia Slater*
Dolores Slater, *Claudia Slater*
Inez Smith, *Marian Smith*

POSEY COUNTY
Audrey Blackburn, *Sharon Sorenson*
& Judy Knowles
Theresa McFadin, *Sharon Sorenson*
& Judy Knowles
Vernell Saltzman, *Sharon Sorenson*
& Judy Knowles
Thelma Roehr, *Sharon Sorenson*

INTERVIEWEE, *INTERVIEWER*

PULASKI COUNTY
Virgie Bowers, *Julia Binkley*
Neva Schlatter, *Julia Binkley*
Mildred Weaver, *Julia Binkley*
Bessie Werner, *Julia Binkley*
Edna Winter, *Julia Binkley*

PUTNAM COUNTY
Marian Job, *Mary Sharp*
Elizabeth McCullough, *Mary Glidewell*

RANDOLPH COUNTY
Valetta Ford, *Helen Symonds*

RIPLEY COUNTY
Ethel Meyer, *Ruth Huneke*
Pearl Snider, *Ruth Huneke*

RUSH COUNTY
Margaret Daubenspeck, *Juanita Rees*
Theresa Fecher, *Juanita Rees*
Kathryn Grinstead, *Eleanor Arnold*
Shirley Morgan, *Virginia Wright*
Marie Weber, *Virginia Wright*

SCOTT COUNTY
Emma Baker, *Doris Prewitt*
Zelma Blocher, *Doris Prewitt &
    Delia Everhart*
Evelyn Buchanan, *Doris Prewitt*
Margaret Dean, *Doris Prewitt*
Opal Whitsett & Juanita Hunter,
    Doris Prewitt & Delia Everhart

SHELBY COUNTY
Mary Ash, *Jewel Luhring*
Mabel Bobbitt, *Jewel Luhring*
Thelma Fox, *Jewel Luhring*
Opal Gallagher, *Jewel Luhring*
Camille Hey, *Eleanor Arnold*

SPENCER COUNTY
Eldo Minor Bell, *Helen Kennedy*

ST. JOSEPH COUNTY
Kathleen Blondia, *Inez Reum*
Helen Marker, *Inez Reum*
Joyce Frederick, *Norma Cline*
Evelyn Koehler, *Norma Cline*
Burnetha Knox, *Norma Cline*

SWITZERLAND COUNTY
Mildred Cochran, *Rachel Hickman*

STEUBEN COUNTY
Margaret Butler, *Virginia Hill*

TIPPECANOE COUNTY
Blanche Martin, *Martha Cox*
Mildred McCay, *Julia Binkley*
Pearl Sollars, *Martha Cox*
Helen Weigle, *Katherine Delaney*

TIPTON COUNTY
Clara Carter, *Elizabeth Barton*

INTERVIEWEE, *INTERVIEWER*

UNION COUNTY
Delpha Borradaile, *Susan McCormick*
Eleanor Cheek, *Susan McCormick*
Bobby Henry, *Susan McCormick*
Phyllis Howard, *Julia Binkley*
Thelma Nixon, *Susan McCormick*
Gleda Stevens, *Susan McCormick*

VANDERBURGH COUNTY
Lulu Rheinhardt, *Mary Herron*
Nancy Schneider, *Lois Appel*
Marie Unfried, *Lois Appel &
    Mary Herron*
Edna Vandenbark, *Lois Appel*

VERMILLION COUNTY
Trilla Alderson, *Marguerite Albright*
Florence Miller, *Marguerite Albright*

VIGO COUNTY
Mable DeWitt, *Marjorie Bedwell*
Beulah Fessant, *Joan Cox*
Thelma Shelburn, *Joan Cox*
Clara Stuthard, *Joan Cox*

WABASH COUNTY
Margaret Garrison, *Louise Dawson*
Alice Guyer, *Louise Dawson*
Mary Johnson, *Louise Dawson*
Alma Knecht, *Louise Dawson*
Clara Nichols, *Louise Dawson*

WASHINGTON COUNTY
Lulie Davis, *Bonnie Pruett*

WAYNE COUNTY
Mary Graver, *Mary Mathews*
Mary Mitchell, *Shirley Wise*
Donna Parker, *Mary Mathews*
Helen Sauser, *Mary Mathews*
Jackie Webb, *Shirley Wise*

WELLS COUNTY
Birdena Day, *Barbara Elliott*
Barbara Elliott, *Birdena Day*
Pearl Gordon, *Birdena Day*
Ruth Grover, *Barbara Elliott*
Fred Park, *Birdena Day*

WHITE COUNTY
Iva Crouse, *Carol Schroeder*
Anna Martin, *Carol Schroeder*
Alene McKinley, *Carol Schroeder*
Doris Stevenson, *Nancy Prue*
Alfreda Wesner, *Carol Schroeder*

WHITLEY COUNTY
Ruby Leedy, *Helen Murbach*
Maggie Owen, *Helen Murbach*
LaVerda Shearer, *Helen Murbach*

Gary ●

South Bend ●

● Fort Wayne

Lafayette ●

Muncie ●

Indianapolis ●

Terre Haute ●

Bloomington ●

● Columbus

Madison ●

● Evansville

LAPORTE · ST. JOSEPH · ELKHART · LAGRANGE · STEUBEN
LAKE · PORTER · NOBLE · DEKALB
MARSHALL · KOSCIUSKO
STARKE · WHITLEY · ALLEN
NEWTON · JASPER · PULASKI · FULTON
WABASH · HUNTING-TON
MIAMI · WELLS · ADAMS
WHITE · CASS
BENTON · CARROLL · GRANT
TIPPE-CANOE · HOWARD · BLACK-FORD · JAY
WARREN · CLINTON · TIPTON · MADISON · DELAWARE · RANDOLPH
FOUNTAIN · MONT-GOMERY · BOONE · HAMILTON · HENRY · WAYNE
PARKE · PUTNAM · HENDRICKS · MARION · HANCOCK · RUSH · FAYETTE · UNION
VERMILLION · VIGO · CLAY · MORGAN · JOHNSON · SHELBY · FRANKLIN
OWEN · DECATUR
SULLIVAN · GREENE · MONROE · BROWN · BARTHO-LOMEW · RIPLEY · DEAR-BORN
JENNINGS · OHIO
KNOX · MARTIN · LAWRENCE · JACKSON · JEFFERSON · SWITZERLAND
DAVIESS · WASHINGTON · SCOTT
ORANGE · CLARK
PIKE · DUBOIS
GIBSON · CRAWFORD · HARRI-SON · FLOYD
POSEY · WARRICK · PERRY
VANDER-BURGH · SPENCER

INDIANA HISTORICAL BUREAU
140 North Senate Avenue
Indianapolis, Indiana